WHO DO YOU
THINK YOU ARE?

WHO DO YOU THINK YOU ARE?

A Devotional on the Book of James

JIM RICHARDS

XULON PRESS

Xulon Press
2301 Lucien Way #415
Maitland, FL 32751
407.339.4217
www.xulonpress.com

Paperback ISBN-13: 978-1-66285-338-8
Ebook ISBN-13: 978-1-66285-339-5

Introduction

As we grow up, we are told things, called things, and do things, both good and bad, that to a large extent form who we are as adults. The good things—the true compliments, the "I love yous," the "congratulations", and so on—we should hang onto. The bad things—the lies, insults, slanders, and emphasized failures— need to be surgically removed, a type of spiritual surgery needs to be done. Both the good and the bad are part of growing up in a fallen world. Both the good and bad also create in us our sense of self-worth or the lack thereof.

As I read the book of James, the Holy Spirit showed me that how I see myself affects how I believe in God and how much confidence I have in Him as I try to figure out this business of serving God, whom I can't see and sometimes have a problem hearing. If my perception of God is of someone with a scowl and a fat thumb just waiting to squash me when I do something wrong, my motivation to serve Him is going to be low to non-existent. But if my understanding of Him allows me to see that He loves me deeply, He will never abandon me, He wants me to have a quality of life I haven't dreamed of, and He will create in me a man who will leave a positive mark in the world and bring glory to His name at the same time, I will be more willing to yield my life to Him, be His servant, and do what He asks me to do.

Who Do You Think You Are started out as my personal notes from reading the Book of James, but as I read and wrote, I thought maybe someone else could benefit from what I learned. My goal through this book is to make you think. My hope is that as you read, you will realize that because God loves you so intensely, you have nothing to fear and eternal life to gain, starting now. I hope you will see that serving God, serving Jesus, is an expression of your love for Him and not a burdensome to-do list. James shows us how to express our love joyfully and live life to the fullest.

For Jay and MariAnne
And all the family.

Thank you.

James 1:1

"James, a bond-servant of God and of the Lord Jesus Christ, To the twelve tribes who are dispersed abroad: Greetings."

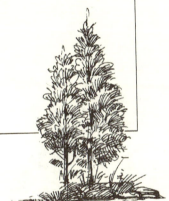

James introduces himself as "a bond-servant of God." The original Greek word for "bond-servant" can also be translated as "servant" or even "slave." What does "bond-servant" mean? Is it just semantics, or is there a difference between being a slave and being a servant?

A *slave,* by definition, is owned property. Someone who is a slave, is legally owned, like a horse or bull, by another individual and expected to work for no pay. In the Biblical East, most slaves were thought of as property. A few were able to gain some rights and even own slaves themselves, but under Roman law most slaves were people owned by their master, without rights and, like any other form of property, could be used and disposed of any way their master chose.

A *servant*, on the other hand, is employed by another person for domestic work or other duties and is recompensed for their work. As Christ's servants, we are people who will receive the compensation of blessings and eternal life for our work for Christ. But while we are called to live in ways that honor God, we will not *earn* anything from Him. Our salvation comes through Jesus and what He did on the cross; His blood paid for our salvation and all that comes with it.

As a Christian, I am both a servant and a slave. I am owned property, bought with the price of Jesus' blood and I belong to Him only. I am also a willing servant of the living God and will be "recompensed" for my work on payday when I stand before the Lord and enter into His kingdom in fulfillment of His promise to me and my trust in Him.

The *bond* part of "bond-servant" indicates a permanent mark, like a brand or an ear notch, voluntarily taken by an individual to identify himself as a lifelong servant of his master. In Scripture, God called his people, the Jews, to take on this kind of bond through circumcision. Any Gentile male, regardless of age, who wanted to become a Jew had to be circumcised. In the

New Covenant brought by Jesus, Christians still take a permanent mark – circumcision of the heart. Paul talks about this in Romans 2:29 and Colossians 2:11. Through the work of the Holy Spirit, our hearts are marked for service to God. It is not a man-made legalistic ritual, but evidence that we serve God from our hearts as a result of His love and mercy toward us!

James essentially calls himself a slave of Christ in this opening line of his letter. What did he mean by that? In James's day, there were a number of ways a person could become a slave. Looking at how someone becomes a slave may help us understand what it means to be a servant of Jesus. Keep in mind while studying the Bible, it's not as much about physical, environmental, or economic poverty as it is about spiritual poverty. So, these ways of becoming a slave apply to us today on a spiritual level. We can be enslaved to sin, or we can be enslaved to Christ. Spiritually, we can be:

1) **Born as slaves.** Children born to slave parents were slaves themselves. All mankind is born in sin. Sin is passed on from generation to generation (Romans 5:12; 6:6, 20). It doesn't matter what our heritage is. It doesn't matter if we think it's fair. Because of what our relatives did in Eden, all people inherit a sin nature and are guilty of sin (Romans 3:23). Sinning comes to us naturally, like breathing. If you want to stop sinning on your own, because you think you don't need this Jesus stuff, stop breathing long enough and you won't sin anymore, but you'll be dead and then it will be too late to change your mind. You can't make yourself holy. You need Jesus.

2) **Captured in war.** Jesus has set us free from sin. As Christians, we are soldiers equipped to fight against sin. But sometimes we can fall back into sin; we are essentially

2

captured or caught up in spiritual battle. Ephesians 6:10-20 first describes the warfare in which we are involved (verse 12), then the armor Christian soldiers of the cross are to put on, and finally, our most powerful weapon (which many Christians seem to think so little of, much to the joy of our enemy, Satan) prayer. Verse 18 says the aggressive Spirit-led warrior must be alert. That is to say we should have our eyes and ears open, and our brains engaged.

3) **Purchased.** As property, slaves could be purchased by one master from another. Parents could also sell their children to escape debt. Even today, whether we are owned by the desire for money, a mirror and a gym membership, or a pimp, we are indeed owned property. The apostle Paul thought he was doing everything right, pleasing God through his ceremonies and persecution of Christians, until God struck him blind and spoke to him (Acts 9). Later, in Romans 7, Paul acknowledges the battle going on inside him between his sinful nature and the desire to please God (Romans 7:14-23). Paul wonders in 7:24, "Who will set me free?" and answers that question in the next verse, saying God will set him free, "through Jesus Christ the Lord!" We who put our faith in Jesus have been purchased by God at the cost of His Son (1 Corinthians 6:19-20). Ephesians 1:7 says we are redeemed by Jesus' blood and receive the forgiveness of our sins by His grace. There is no other way to have a relationship with God (John 14:6).

4) **Debtors.** Those who were bankrupt could find themselves or their children confiscated as slaves to pay a debt (2 Kings 4:1). This is what I think happened in Eden.

Because of the sins committed by Adam and Eve, they lost the inheritance and rights they had as children of the King. By default, all generations from that point have fallen into spiritual poverty and become slaves to sin and Satan. God did not give up and leave us. We turned our backs and blamed Him. We began looking for another "father image" to give us each a sense of security and worth.

5) **Self-sold**. To escape poverty, people could choose to sell themselves. Today, there are people who do this every day and every night on a physical level, but this can be done on a spiritual level as well. We end up paying out much more than we could ever bring in. This kind of poverty has no class or racial barriers. No amount of money can buy you out of it and a lack of money will not put you there. We all decide our self-worth and who or what our master is at some point in our lives—often by not making any decision at all. We decide at a young age what will make us happy. We decide who our mentors will be. We decide how we will run our lives and maybe the lives of those around us. We think if we play our cards right fortune might smile on us because we've been told life's a gamble, right? But, in the end, the house always wins. At what income level will I consider myself to have escaped poverty? What am I worth? How much am I willing to settle for? To whom or to what would I sell my soul (Matthew 16:26)?

The gospel truth is even though we might look good on the outside, we are stinking tombs on the inside (Matthew 23:27; 16:26, 27; 7:15-23). Bob Dylan sang that we all are, "gonna have to serve somebody." So, in the end, a slave is still a slave, right? What's the difference? I'm either a slave to my sin or I'm a slave to God.

If you're like me, you don't want to be slave to anybody. But like it or not, we already are slaves to someone or something. Either we're slaves to Satan, which can mean being a slave to anything tied to this world (like sports, the environment, money, drugs, work etc.) or we're slaves to Jesus, which means pursuing a personal relationship with Him through prayer, Bible study, and meeting with other Christians. It may mean some community service and helping neighbors. The bottom line is this: which life investment is going to give you the best return when you die? You'll have eternal life either way. The kicker is where you spend it: Hell, by serving self, Satan, and the world, leaving Jesus completely out of the picture, or Heaven with Jesus in a place completely free of any sin, sorrow, pain, or suffering. It's your choice.

Before coming to faith in Jesus, I was a nice person. I was also a slave to drug addiction and people's approval. I did some pretty selfish things and deeply hurt a lot of people close to me. Jesus has set me free from the control of those things. Like James, I have chosen to become a bond-servant to Christ instead of to the world. My heart has been permanently marked, and by choice I will die a servant of the Lord and spend my eternity in Heaven.

James 1:2-4

"Consider it all joy, my brethren, when you encounter various trials, knowing that the testing of your faith produces endurance. And let endurance have its perfect result, so that you may be perfect and complete, lacking in nothing."

Sure, count it pure joy when your life falls to pieces. Dance in the street because the bank foreclosed on your house? When you're down with some mysterious disease, when your children are taken from you, when your business fails, when your significant other tells you that they are amazed that they have put up with you for so long, that they would be better off single or dead... Praise the Lord? Is that what you *feel* like doing? No, probably not. More than once I have thought to myself, "Sorry, God, but I'm just not feeling the joy right now... don't feel like talking about it either."

There is a common belief drifting around among many Christians that once you "find Jesus" you will always be happy, never sad, never even get sick, and have everything given to you that you ever want or need. Really, I was told this before I became a believer and I thought, "Jeez, if that's true, a person would have to be an idiot not to become a Christian... forget the Gospel, just tell people they will have everything handed to them, never be sad, and live forever." This is a lie.

Soon after I became a believer, a Christian man whom I loved deeply died. He had a hand in leading me to Jesus. I knew him before he became a believer and lived with his family after he was born again. He taught me by example what a mature Christian man was like and was himself a wonderful example of a born-again father and husband. I learned over the phone one Christmas Eve he had passed away a few months before from cancer. I lost it. I was completely destroyed, overcome by a tidal wave of grief and loss. So, what happened to this joy-of-Jesus? Where was God who said He would never leave me?

Think about what happened to Job. He lost his children, his property, and his health in horrible ways, and then his loving wife tells him, "Are you nuts? Curse God and die! End your suffering! It would be better than living like you are." What was Job's response? "Hey, why didn't I think of that? That's a good idea!" No, Job said, "You speak as if you were a foolish woman. Shall we accept only the good from God *and not the bad*?" (Job 2:9-10, emphasis mine).

Interesting question. Does God *give* us bad stuff to deal with just to see what we will do? Why would God, who loves you, do that?

Later, Job says to his friends, "If He were to slay me, yet I will hope in Him" (Job 13:15). Was Job happy about his situation? No, not at all. In fact, he had cursed the day he was born (Job 3), but he never cursed God. Job knew God was completely sovereign over all things, and he knew God loved him. In fact, this might have been part of his frustration. He couldn't understand why his God would allow all this to happen to him. In the middle of a bad situation, it's hard (sometimes impossible) for us to see how anything good could come out of such pain. But it can. It's hard to understand how a loving God could allow us to go through something like that. We feel completely alone in a vast and dark universe. But He will never actually leave us alone (Joshua 1:5-6; Hebrews 13:5).

According to James 1:3, it is our faith that is being *tested* (tried and purified); it's being made stronger. The Bible is full of evidence that we don't become strong by being isolated from hardship. Strength of character, faith, and godly wisdom grow in tough times. Spend some time studying and praying through Ecclesiastes and 1 Corinthians 10:13 to see you are not the first or only one to struggle. If you look through Romans 8:26-39, you will see that you are not alone in your battles because the Holy Spirit is there with you and in you. Expect tough times to come and realize you will fall at times. But also realize that *nothing* ever separates you from God and His love. I have learned that the more important issue is not who you are when the hard times hit, but who you become when you come out the other side. If you hang onto Jesus, study the Bible, and trust Him through the trials, your faith will grow, and you will become a stronger soldier. But, if you allow yourself to wallow in darkness, trying to fix things on your own without His word, His direction, or His power, it will only get darker. So, to a large degree, gaining greater strength or remaining in weakness, experiencing victory or resigning to defeat is up to you. There is power in the name of Jesus, and we have the choice to claim that power or reject it in favor of relying on our own weakness.

Look at John 15:1-5 –

> "I am the true vine, and My Father is the vine-dresser. Every branch in Me that does not bear fruit, He takes away; and every branch that bears fruit, He prunes it so that it may bear more fruit. You are already clean because of the word which I have spoken to you. Abide in Me, and I in you. As the branch cannot bear fruit of itself unless it abides in the vine, so neither can you unless you abide in Me. I am the vine, you are the branches; he who abides in Me and I in him, he bears much fruit, for apart from Me you can do nothing."

How would God "prune" you, the branch? One way might be by allowing "trials" to come your way. Why? So, your faith will be made stronger, so that you will bear much fruit. And according to Hebrews 11:6, the only way a person can bear fruit (that is, please God), is obeying through faith.

Why would I want to please a God who says He loves me, yet still allows me to go through some really bad stuff, or doesn't protect me from it? Why should I continue to try when I know it's possible that it won't get any easier? And why would I want to be a "stronger" Christian if I can get into Heaven regardless of how strong my faith is? In a nutshell, because it's worth it; your return on investment far exceeds any sacrifice. Paul says in Philippians 3:8 that he considers all the hard times and things lost as dung when compared to the excellence of knowing and having a relationship with Jesus. If you really love somebody, you will naturally do things to please them, not because you have to but because you want to. Not wanting to, or not trying to be a stronger Christian is akin to marrying someone then leaving your spouse the first time difficulties arise. Love is patient and endures all things (1 Corinthians 13). As a result of enduring, that love, that person, and that relationship all become stronger.

So, let's refocus. Instead of dwelling on how bad the situation might be, or how you're going to try and get yourself out of it, remember that Jesus uses all situations for your benefit and His glory. It is like undergoing physical therapy, don't focus on the pain, as bad as it may be, focus on how the Therapist is going to get you through the pain. Be faithful in following His instructions. Working through this with Him and in His timing will not only cause you to grow in faith, become stronger in heart, and see the victory He brings, but the people around you will see God's work in you and His work through you as well (Matthew 5:16). Remember Job asking, "Should we accept only the good from God, *and not the bad*"? Even the best parents know that they cannot (and should not) protect their children from all the hardship that life throws at them any more than they can protect them from a cold or flu. Obviously, protecting kids from dangerous situations is a parent's job; parents should know where to draw the line. Yet children need to be exposed to hardships to get stronger and have more endurance to deal with them more successfully as they grow. Children are able to get through scary situations when they know their parents love them and are there with them through the tough times. We can have confidence and joy through trying times because our God, our Father who loves us and never leaves us, is with us through it all.

James 1:3-4

"Knowing that the testing of your faith produces endurance and let endurance have its perfect result, so that you may be perfect and complete, lacking in nothing."

Knowing that the testing of my faith produces endurance. Am I supposed to know that this testing, this thing God is allowing to happen, is going to produce more endurance? Am I supposed to know this *beforehand*? Yes—that's why it is so important to have a tight hold on your conviction of who God is and to know His character. Earlier, we discussed if you think that God is in Heaven just waiting for you to do something wrong so He can squash you, then doubt is immediately going to fill your head when these temptations and trials come along. On the other hand, if you have put on the armor of God (Ephesians 6:1-17) and if you know beyond doubt that He is your loving Father, holy God, and Protector, you will also know, one way or another, He will get you through it.

Does that mean He's going to tempt us to sin in order to make us practice perseverance? No. There is a big difference between *tempting* and *testing*. Temptation is, by its nature, founded on deceit. You'll never read in Scripture where God tempts anyone. Temptation means we are being drawn or lured away from Jesus, our source of strength and protection, by Satan or our own lusts to do something we know is wrong (James 1:13-16). Satan's temptations appeal to our pride, then he guilts us into feeling defeated, worthless, and unloved by God. God allows our faith to be tested (or tried) for the purpose of drawing us closer to Him. At the same time the Holy Spirit makes our faith stronger, producing endurance that enables us to do more and greater things (John 14:12ff). A growing, stronger faith implies there has been action on our part as the Spirit leads us.

In Matthew 16:15-16, Jesus asks Peter who he thinks He is. Peter says Jesus is "the Christ, the Son of the living God." Peter has essentially professed faith in Jesus as his Lord and Savior, just like you and I can today. I wonder how convinced Peter was when he professed Jesus' true identity. Evidently, Satan didn't think Peter's faith would stand up under trial. In Luke

22:31, Jesus advises Peter that his faith exercise program will begin sooner than he expects. Jesus tells him that Satan has demanded to sift Peter like wheat, but that Jesus has prayed Peter's faith will not fail. Notice that Jesus did not pray that Peter's trials would go away. Now, how did Jesus know about Satan's demands? Jesus and the Father are One (John 10:30; 17:21). Satan had to ask (demand) permission before he had any access to Peter at all. Doesn't it stand to reason that Satan can do nothing that God does not allow, and if God allows it to happen, then He will be there with us though it all?

Peter's trials involved watching Jesus being arrested and put to death. How would Peter respond in these trials? In Matthew 26:51, in an effort to protect Jesus from His arrestors, Peter draws his sword and cuts off the ear of one of the men. Jesus tells him to put the sword away. In Matthew 26:69-74, Peter vehemently denies even knowing Jesus when questioned by a little girl. Matthew 26:75 records that at his last denial (of three), he ran away and wept bitterly. It seems that Peter was having some trials here, and not too much joy.

But in Acts 2, something happened in that upper room, something big. The Holy Spirit came like fire and wind, filling Peter and the other disciples with the third member of the Godhead. Suddenly, we see their faith grow and their relationship with God deepen as they become obedient to the Holy Spirit's leading. Peter did not have the Holy Spirit in him until this point; he acted and spoke according to his passions and emotions of the moment. After the coming of the Spirit, Peter and the other apostles rejoiced in God's grace and faithfulness, even though many of them faced persecution and even lost their lives as a result of their service to God. The Holy Spirit's work in them transformed their trials into enduring faith.

In Matthew 16:16-18, Jesus told Peter that "upon this rock I will build My church; and the gates of Hades will not overpower it." God was building His church on Peter's *faith*, not on the man. Peter was human like you and me, and humans are fallible. We are strong one minute and running like a bunny the next, kind of like Peter (John 18:17-27). We make impressive promises and manage to keep some of them, kind of like Peter (Mark 14:29-30; John 16:32). The fact that God is building His church—which includes you and me—on God-given faith and not on the "goodness" of humanity or human performance is quite reassuring to me. True faith, the ability and willingness to believe God at all, is from God, and faith's foundation is the finished work of Jesus on the cross and the promises of God in Scripture. We cannot generate it ourselves because our sinful nature cannot produce anything righteous. Everything that comes from Him is perfect and constant (James 1:17). What happens to our faith after we get it is up to us. Through believing God and acting on His leading, our faith will grow to massive strength. We can nurture our faith through trusting obedience, giving God glory and praise, or we can allow it to wither through faithless disobedience.

A major personal renovation may be needed to bring a person closer to Jesus, but God is interested in building faith up and not in breaking people down. God always works through trials to offer us a closer relationship with Him and to bring us closer to our full potential. He always works with each person's best interests and His glorification in mind. In Acts 2, after the Holy Spirit had entered the apostles, they began praising God and speaking in tongues (foreign languages). People around them who had witnessed this began saying the apostles were drunk, mocking them. But Peter, like Peter often did, immediately stood up and started talking. However, *unlike* what Peter often did, he spoke boldly and rationally, quoting the prophets regarding Jesus, recounting how the people had just crucified the Son of God, and as a result of God's message through Peter, about three thousand people were baptized.

Our "Acts 2 moment" happens at the instant we believe the Gospel and yield our lives to Jesus. The Holy Spirit within us never changes. What changes, matures, and grows in beauty and potency is our trust and our confidence in Him as we follow Him through the dark valleys. We often get swept up in worry and fear. God doesn't worry about that stuff or anything. He dealt with it at Calvary.

I have often thought, prayed, and wished that I had the same confidence in God that He has in me. He created me, so He knows exactly what I am capable of. I am specially designed for a specific purpose. and so are you. How far out on the limb are we willing to go? Are we willing to maybe get a little dirty or follow Jesus through the mud, to come out stronger with more endurance on the other side? Are we willing to trust that God's testing will produce the endurance our faith needs?

All too often, I try to avoid tribulations. I try to avoid confrontation or hardship. I mean, nobody actually *wants* bad times, do they? But James says to allow "endurance to have its perfect result, that you may be mature, complete, lacking in nothing."

People who are in an exercise program find they have more endurance after participating than when they started because they were faithful with their diets and did what the trainer told them. They look back at how hard it was then and marvel at what they are capable of doing now. Working through hardship indeed produces endurance. Following a good trainer, like Jesus, produces good results. Following a bad trainer can get you hurt.

When we start the exercise class or when we enter a trial, we too often pray that He will deliver us from the pain. James focuses not on the pain, but on the result of faithfully enduring and remaining faithful through the trial: perfection and completion. All of Scripture, from Genesis through the Revelation, is the story of God our Father calling us back from our sinful, stubborn rebellion to peace with Him. Our return journey is not easy. (John Bunyan's *Pilgrim's Progress* illustrates the journey faithful followers of Jesus go through.)

In Jeremiah 17:7-8, God promises that He will bless those who trust Him. Romans 5:1-5 says that we can find joy in tribulation because the perseverance we show brings proven character which brings hope, that joyful, expectant confidence for the future!

We can know beyond doubt, based on God's word, that if we faithfully trust God through our toughest times, He is there with us. By remaining true to the end, we will be stronger in faith when we come out the other side!

James 1:5-8

"But if any of you lacks wisdom, let him ask of God, who gives to all generously and without reproach, and it will be given to him. But he must ask in faith without any doubting, for the one who doubts is like the surf of the sea, driven and tossed by the wind. For that man ought not to expect that he will receive anything from the Lord, being a double-minded man, unstable in all his ways."

To have wisdom means that you make good use of knowledge, often gained through life experience. To have godly wisdom means that God has taught you something about Himself or yourself (again, often through experiences) and now you are able to make sound choices based on what you have learned from God.

Coming on the heels of James's encouragement to persevere, verse 5 starts with "But, if you lack wisdom," which implies to be successful in enduring trials and navigating tough circumstances, we need godly wisdom. It doesn't matter if you have been a Christian twenty minutes or twenty years; there are going to be times when you simply don't understand what to do, what God is doing, or even where He is. *Maybe I crossed the line once too many times... maybe He wasn't really with me to begin with...* Don't listen to lies like these ever, because you're doubting God's promise. You're being double-minded. Hebrews 13:5 promises that "I [the Lord] will never leave you or forsake you." He will not leave you stranded or give up on you, ever. Proverbs 1:7 and 9:10 tell us that the worship and admiration ("fear") of the Lord are the beginning of wisdom. These are evidences of wisdom. We take our eyes off of ourselves and our failures and trust God instead. The great prophet Clint Eastwood once said, "A man's gotta know his limits," but God is limitless. So, trust Jesus. Ask Him for wisdom. Not only does He have your back, He has your soul.

Through Jesus we have the ability, the opportunity, and the privilege to have an intimate, personal relationship with the Creator and Sustainer of the universe, who deeply loves and cares for us no matter what our circumstances look like. Satan preys on our uncertainties and our doubts. If we allow him to, he will multiply them and magnify them to the point where we are drowning, tossed by the wind in every direction, not knowing what to believe. If people allow themselves to get into this situation, is it any wonder they will not receive anything from the

Lord? It's not that the Lord is withholding anything from them, they simply cannot or will not accept what He is offering. In their minds, they have too much conflicting information. To them, it seems that His Truth doesn't make sense for their situation. There must be another way, they think. There isn't, and Satan knows this. Can God overcome your doubt? Not unless you're willing to trust the God you can't see to do things you can't understand; your doubt can become unbelief.

Imagine a child climbs a tree then discovers he can't get down. The boy calls for help and his father comes to lift him down. Glad to help, the father reaches up, but by refusing to let go of the tree, the boy cannot reach for the arms of his father. Unless the boy lets go of the tree and trusts his father, how can he receive any help? The boy is double-minded, wanting help but doubting the ability of his father, unwilling to trust him (see Mark 9:17-29, especially verses 23 and 24). If pleasing God comes only through trusting Him (John 15:4-5), then it stands to reason that a double-minded person would be unstable in all attempts to please God. Romans 8:5-8 and Hebrews 11:6 also testify about the importance of single-mindedness in serving our Lord.

In 1 Kings 3:5-9, Solomon, then a young man, was king of Israel. God said to him in a dream, "Ask what you wish me to give you." Solomon could have asked for and received anything from God. But, instead of power, wealth, or the death of his enemies, Solomon asked for wisdom, an understanding heart to discern between good and evil: "For who is able to judge [govern] this great people of yours?" God was very pleased. If Solomon had asked for wealth or power or anything else God would have given it to him because He said He would. And Solomon could have immediately fallen into worshipping those things instead of learning how to manage them and governing the people of Israel.

Unfortunately, having wisdom doesn't make us immune to making bad decisions. Later in life, Solomon did, indeed, become ridiculously wealthy and began to worship his power and wealth. So, did God give Solomon riches and power knowing that it would cause him to falter? He did give him those gifts, but we can't blame God for that any more than we can blame God for trouble we get ourselves into while misusing any gifts or talents that God may have given us. We have taken our eyes off the Giver and fixed them on the gift instead.

As James reminds us (verse 6), we must ask for wisdom in complete faith, trusting God without doubt, and it will be given generously! Hebrews 4:16 tells us that through prayer we can go directly into the presence of God with confidence to receive mercy and grace any time. There is never a need to pray to anyone or anything else. Luke 11:10-13 says God withholds no good thing from us. We can never completely understand God or some of the reasons He does what He does, but we don't have to. Godly wisdom tells us that there is peace beyond understanding when we trust Him and His ways and rely on His methods instead of our own. This trust creates within us the single-mindedness we need to be at peace with both ourselves and God, making us able to receive anything that He, or life, might throw at us.

James 1:9-12

"But the brother of humble circumstances is to glory in his high position; and the rich man is to glory in his humiliation, because like flowering grass he will pass away. For the sun rises with a scorching wind and withers the grass; and its flower falls off and the beauty of its appearance is destroyed; so too the rich man in the midst of his pursuits will fade away. Blessed is a man who preserves under trial; for once he has been approved, he will receive the crown of life which the Lord has promised to those who love Him."

James is addressing two kinds of people here, reminding us that a person's single-minded focus must be on what true riches are and where they lie (Matthew 6:19-24). First, let the poor find unlimited comfort in knowing that their true riches and high position are not in this world, but in their heavenly Father's Kingdom above. That's wisdom. Secondly, the godly rich must realize the riches they have here are not theirs but God's riches on loan to them, for which they are accountable. Believers with worldly wealth must also realize the riches stored in Heaven have an eternal value far exceeding any wealth the world offers.

Rich or poor, all people will die, but all who are heirs with Christ will be seated together in the banquet hall of Heaven. We, all together, rich and poor, are one in Christ. That's glorious.

Without Jesus, both the rich person and the poor person will fade away like the flowering grass in the middle of their striving with their own agendas. The poor man focuses on trying to make ends meet or live the "good life" by spending beyond his income while trying to keep up with his rich neighbor, who, truthfully, is doing the same thing. Both of them have fallen prey to the world's temptations and lies, not finding peace by looking to God, who will provide for all their needs.

In Mark 10:25, Jesus gives the example of it being easier for a camel to pass through the eye of a needle than for a rich man to enter Heaven. Here in James, the rich man will "fade away," not because he's rich, but because the things he's pursuing have taken the place of God, as they did for Solomon. For such a person, *things* become his god. He worships the creation rather than the Creator (Romans 1:25). Being rich or wealthy is not a sin, nor does it automatically or inevitably lead to sin. Fading away may or may not mean actually dying (separated forever from God), though for the unbelieving person that would, indeed, be true. But believers can also "fade away" while living on earth. As believers, we are "children of light" and we should be in constant fellowship with God, living in His light (Ephesians 5:8). But if we allow our priorities to get out of order, we begin to live our lives in darkness. Our spirits within us get their nutrition from the word of God, just like plants turn sunlight into energy to absorb the nutrients of the soil (Matthew 4:4). As plants without sufficient sunlight wilt and fade, if we limit the light of God's presence by neglecting fellowship with Him and other Christians or exposure to Scriptural learning, we will fade away like the flowers of the field. Our testimony will be weakened. Our desire to grow will fail. Our ministry will flounder. Our joy will fade. Guaranteed.

Our economic level has nothing to do with God's economy. Having or not having wealth is not the issue. The issue is the attitude toward wealth and how it is dealt with. And you will deal with it in much the same manner that you deal with any other trial or temptation. Do you worry and get stressed about the situation? *How do I fix this problem and still look like I know what I'm doing?* Do you blame others? *If it weren't for them, I wouldn't be in this mess.* Or do you search for Jesus and His wisdom and direction regardless of what the outcome might be? Is personal integrity and character as important to you as wealth? What is *wealth* to you? Having wealth is having an abundance (much more than needed) of something that you consider valuable. I may consider good soil valuable, or guns, or old books, or cars. Someone else might find those things worthless. Wealth, like beauty, is in the eye of the beholder. Do I consider my relationship with Jesus as valuable as the earthly things I will leave behind when I die?

In Revelation 2:9-11, Jesus addresses the "poor" but faithful church at Smyrna. He starts His letter to them by reassuring them of who He is: "The first and last, who was dead, and has come to life." The resurrected Lord of Lords say to them,

"I know your tribulation and your poverty (but you are rich), and the blasphemy by those who say they are Jews and are not, but are a synagogue of Satan. Do not fear what you are about to suffer. Behold, the devil is about to cast some of you into prison, so that you will be tested, and you will have tribulation for ten days. Be faithful until death, and I will give you the crown of life. He who has an ear, let him hear what the Spirit says to the churches. He who overcomes will not be hurt by the second death."

It's interesting that Jesus knows their poverty, but says that they are *rich*. Apparently what Jesus sees as their wealth is invisible to them. In God's economy, putting our faith in Him and serving Him stores up riches in Heaven that far exceed any bank account here. Life in this world is filled with all kinds of hardships and persecution. But stay faithful, trust Jesus until death, and He will give you the crown of life (James 1:13). Though our bodies die, we will be rewarded with eternal life, living forever with our Lord Jesus in His kingdom!

James 1:13

*"Let no one say when he is tempted,
'I am being tempted by God;' for
God cannot be tempted by evil, and
He Himself does not tempt anyone."*

Hard times, tribulations, and trials, are simply a part of being alive. They happen to everybody. Even Jesus had bad days, but He didn't sin, which brings up the point of the difference between being involved in a *trial* and being a victim of *temptation*.

In Mark 1 and Matthew 4, Jesus was in the wilderness being tempted by Satan, who was trying to get Jesus to do things that would thwart His reason for being there. Why was Jesus in the middle of nowhere in the first place? Let's back up a step, why did Jesus come to Earth in the first place? He came to bring the Gospel of salvation, to be visible proof of the love of God for His people, to be the perfect and final sacrifice for the sin of all humanity, and to permanently break the chains of sin that Satan held us by. The scope of His mission required Him to take drastic steps in preparation—forty days of prayer and fasting alone in the desert. We could easily say that those days, even for Jesus, were hard, trying times, which Satan tried to take advantage of without success. Satan approached Jesus on the fortieth day and asked him to turn bread into stone (Matthew 4:2). Jesus must have been pretty hungry by then, so what would be so bad about turning a rock into a piece of bread? Nobody would know, right? Wrong. Jesus would know that He fell victim to the enemy's temptation. He would have done the will of the deceiver. He would have failed to prepare himself for the purpose He came for. He would no longer be the spotless lamb needed for the sacrifice for the sins of the world. Jesus would have sinned. Satan would have won. We would have been lost forever. This encounter with Satan in the desert was one of Jesus' *trials*, yet he did not sin by falling victim to Satan's *temptation*.

In the middle of our trials, we have the choice to do what we know is right in spite of how we feel. We don't have to follow the leadings of our enemy, Satan. The choice is ours, and the results from those choices will be ours to bear as well. God, who is the great Healer, loving Father and righteous Judge, will never tempt you to sin because the result of our sin is separation from Him. If there were evil in God, who is all-powerful and eternal, no thinking person would even consider that they could find eternal peace and tranquility with Him. That would make no sense. Why and how would a God who had evil within Him demand complete righteousness from us, an already sinful people? Why would a God like that sacrifice His only son as payment for holiness He doesn't have Himself? There is neither evil nor deception in God. He cannot tempt us to do anything evil. God does allow us to go through trials, but He does not lead us into them by temptation.

James 1:14-17

"But each one is tempted when he is carried away and enticed by his own lust. Then when lust has conceived, it gives birth to sin; and when sin is accomplished, it brings forth death. Do not be deceived my beloved brethren. Every good thing bestowed, and every perfect gift is from above, coming down from the Father of lights, with whom there is no variation, no shifting shadow. In the exercise of His will He brought us forth by the word of truth, so that we would be a kind of first fruits among His creatures. This you know, my beloved brethren."

So, if God doesn't tempt us to sin, where does that temptation come from? James tells us our own lusts tempt us. Lust is a passionate, deceptive, overmastering desire, or craving. Often, we think of it only regarding sex, but it can encompass much more than that—the desire for power, control, money, recognition, food, work, or physical fitness, for example. Sometimes lust goes by other names, like "the drive to achieve." Lust and greed go hand-in-hand, and Satan takes advantage of our lusts to carry us into sin. This is what happened to Adam and Eve in the Garden of Eden. Satan told them partial truths to stir up their curiosity and their desire, which, in disobedience, turned to lust. As a result, they fell into sin, and that sin resulted in their eventual physical death, the loss of their perfect connection with God, and because we inherited their sinful nature caused our separation from God as well.

The strategies of lust and greed still work today, so Satan still uses them today. As the saying goes, "If it works, don't fix it." He brings up an object of our desire and gives us only select information to fuel our greed, encouraging us to make decisions and do things that lead us away from God. This strategy of Satan's allows us to believe that we are masters of our own destinies, making decisions that we think are exercises of our independence and empowerment and then later finding that we are paying the price of those decisions.

In other words, Satan takes advantage of our own lusts to lead us to think God withholds good gifts from us. James says the idea that God is holding out on us should be our first clue that something's not right. If the things we want are truly that important for us, God will provide them. Maybe now, maybe later, but good and perfect gifts always come from God.

Let's consider this question: does Satan tempt us with good gifts? What if a seemingly good gift turns into a source of temptation? Does that make God responsible for our temptation? No.

If a temptation arises, the gift isn't the source of the temptation—the problem is how we react to receiving it and using it. Do we allow our pride or Satan to manipulate us through it? Any gift is an opportunity. It could be a ring, a car, a promotion, whatever. When a gift is presented to us, we consider who the giver is and why the giver gave it to us. Let's say you receive a promotion. God might give it to you because He knows you will honor His name in and through that position. That is not to say that you will be free from tribulation during this time, but your relationship with God will grow as a result of your faithfulness through it all. His motives are good, and His gift is good and perfect. Meanwhile, Satan might try to twist or distort this gift by moving your eyes off of God. He might tease your pride into thinking you can do it alone, so the times you look for God's help or guidance grow fewer and further apart. As a result, you might struggle to perform the work. You might do the job well, but have increasing stress in your family life, or compromise your relationships with friends or even with God Himself in pursuit of the gift God gave you. Satan's motive is always, in the end, to destroy you and throw dirt on God's name. Why does God allow Satan to do that? Again, the promotion itself is not the issue. How we handle getting the promotion and how we allow it to change us are the issues. God would use the experience to make our faith stronger and bring us closer to Him. Satan would use it to puff our pride up, break our faith down, and lure us away from God.

Think back to Solomon. God gifted him with wisdom as he asked God to do. The gift of wisdom was a good and perfect gift, but Solomon allowed his lusts to get in the way of his ability to rule the people. In the end, lust leads to sin, which leads to separation from God, which leads to death (James 1:15).

James 1:18-19a

"In the exercise of His will He brought us forth by the word of truth, so that we would be a kind of first fruits amount His creatures. This you know, my beloved brethren."

Before Genesis, God was all that existed. In all his fullness He needed nothing. Yet, He wanted to have company with us and share all that He is with us. Even after the fall from grace in Eden, His desire never changed. God has not changed. Our Father in Heaven longs to be intimately involved with us. But, because of our sin, He can't. His righteousness and holiness cannot have company with our sin. God was not going to let our sin forever separate us from him, and because of our sin, His justice demanded blood be shed to make atonement to cover sin (Leviticus 6:1-7 and John 1:29). But God took atonement a step further. To show the value He puts on human life and the magnitude of His desire for each one of us, He allowed His only son Jesus to be beaten and crucified as a blood sacrifice for our sin. Jesus was the last sacrifice for all the sin of all humanity! Our opportunity for salvation is a gift provided by God through the death and resurrection of His son Jesus. We cannot earn our salvation, nor can we repay God for what He did (Romans 8, especially verses 3 and 4). God has not changed (James 1:17 reminds us God does not vary or change), and neither has His desire and adoration for us. Salvation is a free gift to those who admit they are sinners and have asked Jesus to forgive their sin and then follow Him by faith.

So, what does it mean to be "brought forth" by the word of truth? Look at Genesis chapter one, when God "brought forth" or created the entire world by the words He spoke. When you became a Christian, you were "brought forth" from the crowd because somehow you heard the Gospel and believed it. Right then you were born again. At your baptism, you are lowered into the water as a person dying to sin and then raised up out of the water alive in Christ; you are "brought forth" as a new creation, presenting yourself to God the Father by faith in His son, Jesus Christ.

Our Father of Lights, who is forever the same, brings us forth as new creations, evidence of His grace and glory and mercy. When I reflect on my life as a Christian and think of all the times I have sinned and "fallen short of the glory of God" (Romans 3:23), I am awestruck that God loves me and chose me in Christ before the foundation of the world to be holy and without blame as I, and as we, stand before Him in love (Ephesians 1:4)!

As you grow in Christ, as your faith matures through reading the Bible, prayer, and life experience, you will see a difference in the way you approach life and its joys and hardships. Others will notice a change in you as well. Why not share the Good Gift with them? You do not have to be a biblical scholar or have all the answers, just tell them what you know and don't make it complicated. People in the world are dying to find true peace. Apart from Jesus, they will simply continue to die, never having found what they needed. Only in Jesus do we have the means to have peace through anything that comes along. Will every situation that we are confronted with throughout our lives turn out in our favor? Probably not. But instead of asking God to explain why tough things are happening the way they are, ask Him for wisdom and the faith to follow Him through it all, and He will give it (James 1:5). Remember, however, when and how God answers is entirely up to Him. Trust Him. He loves you. Sometimes things happen that we will never understand this side of Heaven. Remember, God is good, and He always redeems your experiences, good and bad, always for your benefit, always for His glory, and always at the perfect time.

James 1:19-21

"But everyone must be quick to hear, slow to speak and slow to anger; for the anger of man does not achieve the righteousness of God. Therefore, putting aside all filthiness and all that remains of wickedness, in humility receive the word implanted, which is able to save your souls."

Being eager to listen and slow to speak have become lost arts. Social media gives thousands of people, who don't know you, instant opportunities to chime in with their solutions and advice on what they "know" you should do. Even in person, we often are so busy forming our replies while our friends are still speaking that we don't really hear all of what they're saying. We're *hearing* them, but not really *listening* to them. The old adage "God gave us two ears and one mouth for a reason" is true. Listen. Think and pray, then speak if needed. There's nothing wrong with a pause in conversation while considering an answer. Maybe if we spent more time trying to really understand what the speaker is trying to say we would be able to reply with a more constructive and thoughtful comment instead of something flippant or even hurtful. Polonius from Shakespeare's *Hamlet* summarizes it this way, "Give every man thy ear, but few thy voice" (Act I, Sc. 3).

According to James, I should not speak impulsively, but rather speak the truth in love. I must be slow to get angry. I should focus on listening and understanding as clearly as possible what the other person is trying to communicate and why. I should consider if I should be involved in the issue or not. I should be eager to listen. Our God does that well. We should too; someday we might need someone to listen to us.

Scripture never says not to get angry. God gets angry. But the Lord does say we are not to act as we did prior to becoming Christians (Ephesians 4:17-32). Ephesians 4:26 tells us it's okay to get angry, but warns us, "in your anger do not sin." We must put aside our old ways, which are "corrupted by the lusts of deceit" (Ephesians 4:22). It is interesting to consider how that happens, that old uncontrolled desire creeps back in. I can always justify my behavior in my eyes just by saying I was angry (after all, that's just the way I am, right?), but that doesn't justify my anger. We are to act in a new way because our mind is being renewed by the Spirit (Ephesians 4:23, Romans 12:2). James 1:20 says our normal, human anger does not achieve the righteousness of God. Our sin-nature gets in the mix-of-the-moment and as a result nothing righteous, that is nothing that pleases God, is ever accomplished.

It's often not easy to remain calm in tense situations. So, the need for our minds to be renewed through the word of God and our humble submission to the Holy Spirit should be obvious. Humbly submitting to the Holy Spirit often means we admitting our way of doing something was wrong, or at least inappropriate to the situation. We must now act in a way that does not come naturally to us. We must confess that His ways are better than ours as we learn in Scripture and act on it. In this time of protest and anger, let's show the world around us the truth-with-grace that Jesus has shown us and introduce them to Love that can save their souls.

James 1:22

"But prove yourselves doers of the word, and not merely hearers who delude themselves."

Imagine there was to be a seminar in your town, and the speaker was going to share methods that would guarantee positive, life-changing results. You probably don't have to imagine very hard or long as these people come around pretty often. But what if this guy had methods that really worked and had been proven effective by generations of people who practiced them for thousands of years? But wait, there's more! What if these methods not only changed your present life, but life after death as well! And that's not all! They could also have a positive influence on the people around you! All you have to do is study the book and put into practice what you are shown.

Imagine you run straight to that seminar, gobble up the speaker's words, eagerly purchase the book, rush home with it, and ... never open it. It sits on your shelf—perhaps even in a prominent position—and grandly collects dust. A year later, you hear that your friend is all excited and planning to attend this speaker's seminar. "Forget it," you say, "It doesn't work! I went to the seminar and bought the book, but my life is still exactly as before."

If you get the book, but never seriously read it or practice what it teaches, how can you or any other reasonable person expect to see any results? The person who simply hears the Speaker's message but does not look intently into the Book or practice the Teaching will go away unchanged. If we call ourselves Christians, go to church, and even tithe, yet the people in the church or the world around us can see no visible, lasting change in our attitude toward others, our language, or our habits, it is possible that we are not followers of Jesus, but only religious hypocrites, who are fooling (deluding) ourselves. We impose a misleading belief on ourselves.

Often, this self-delusion comes from going through all the "right" motions. Some may believe that clocking into a Sunday service or attending a weekly Bible study group takes the place of reading and studying the Bible personally or submitting to a more scripturally mature person. These are good steps, but James is calling us to live our faith with integrity—consistency between our beliefs, words, and actions. To be people of integrity, we need to spend quality time alone with our heavenly Father in addition to getting to know Him in group settings.

Men and women of integrity build on the solid foundation of Jesus by acting on the Word of God through the leading of the Holy Spirit, both in public ministry and personal life. This is being a doer of the word. To be merely a hearer of the word is to not allow the Spirit to build you into the person God intended and created you to be. A hearer will probably know what the Bible says but deny its power. A hearer will probably be satisfied with being a good person.

Jesus wants and deserves more than just a few minutes out of your day. If He is the Lord of your life, it should be of your entire life and your entire day. Is His Lordship affecting the way you do business, the quality of your work, how you relate with neighbors and friends, and how you treat your family? Matthew 7:24-29 gives the example of two men who built houses, one on rock and one on the sand. It's a story about building on solid foundations and about developing integrity in life on the foundation of Jesus. The person who built on the rock (the Word, the Cornerstone) withstood the storms of life and maintained integrity. The individual's house built on a sandy foundation (anything other than God's Word, such as our good intentions, self-confidence, reputation, etc.) fell in the storm with a loud crash and that person lost whatever integrity may have been there.

Obadiah 1:3-4 cautions us about how we build our houses—that is to say, how we live our lives. In our pride and self-confidence, it can become easy for us to take our eyes away from God and His Word and think that the works we do are pleasing to Him when they really are done to make us look good and godly.

Our own sin has deceived us. God's word in Micah 6:8 gives the simple solution on how to be doers of the word, "Do justice, love kindness, and walk humbly with your God."

For more consideration of integrity in our words, lifestyle, and testimony, refer to John 14:15, 21; John 15:10; 1 John 2:3-4, 1 John 3:22-24; 1 John 5:2-4; 2 John 6, and Hebrews 4:7-16.

James 1:23-25

"For if anyone is a hearer of the word and not a doer, he is like a man who looks at his natural face in a mirror; for once he has looked at himself and gone away, he has immediately forgotten what kind of person he was. But one who looks intently at the perfect law of liberty, and abides by it, not having become a forgetful hearer but an effectual doer, this man shall be blessed in what he does."

Who are you down inside? It's not about your job or your family. Who are *you*? What do you think of the person you see in the mirror? Why? Believe it or not, this is important.

What is the mirror in this verse? It's Scripture, illuminated by the Holy Spirit. The mirror shows who you actually are, and it may not reflect what you believe about yourself. The verse says that people who are serious about Scripture and seeking godliness see what the mirror shows them. The two different persons described in verses 24 and 25 make infinitely important decisions here. When confronted with the truth of the Gospel, the person in verse 24 is shown personal sin and guilt before God, the need for repentance, and the penalty for not repenting. Since God's truth is always balanced and complete, this person is also shown God's mercy, love, and grace, as well as His perfectly just nature. At this point, peer-pressure, Satan's lies, and possibly simple unconcern may cause the person to disregard what the mirror shows and walk away. Failure to willfully make a decision either for or against God is the same as rejecting Him and His gift of salvation.

In verse 25, we see another person confronted with God's truth in the Gospel. This person also sees what the mirror is showing, but this person looks intently through the lens of the Gospel. People like this see themselves as God sees them and continue to see themselves that way. During their learning and maturing process, they allow the Holy Spirit to reach inside and do His heart-renovation work (1 Thessalonians 5:19).

The Holy Spirit renews our mind when we regularly and intently look into the Word of God (Psalm 119:9-16). To look *intently* into Scripture means to pray and ask Jesus to give you understanding. Without the help and teaching of the Holy Spirit, the full truth and power of the Bible cannot be understood (1 Corinthians 1:18-2:16). But with renewed minds, we begin to worship God through our daily actions (Romans 12:1-2) because we remember what type of people we were and to what we were condemned. Now, in gratitude, we show God our love and appreciation for what Jesus has done through our works (2 Corinthians 5:14-15). When we love people, we want to do things for them that show them our love. We do the same with God.

When you look at the people in the Bible, how do you compare yourself? We all do this. We read about Daniel in the den of lions and suddenly we wonder what we would do in there. Or what about Adam, Eve, Esther, Moses, Samson, Peter, or Judas Iscariot? How do you see yourself? Ineffectual, confused, afraid, or guilty all the time? Do you see yourself as having too little faith before God, or as a pawn of the Fates? Or do you really believe what Scripture says—what God says—about you? Do you see yourself as a resurrected soldier of the cross whose sins have all been forgiven? Righteous only by faith, you are now a strong, battle-scarred new creation in Christ, filled with the Holy Spirit, that third person of the Holy Trinity! You, only through Jesus and His blood that was shed for you, have full communion with God through prayer!

Our enemy will continually attack you, accuse you, and point out every weakness you have in an effort to demoralize you, discredit you, hinder you, and destroy your ministry or family. Stand firmly against his attacks on the solid foundation of faith in Jesus, having put on the full armor of Christ (Romans 13:12; Ephesians 6:11).

When you encounter the living Word of God, you come to a crossroad. In one direction, you continue through life (and death) hopelessly bound to sin and Satan to spend eternity in Hell separated from God. In the other direction, you acknowledge what God says to be true—that you are a sinner and need to be cleansed from your sin by the blood of Christ by faith in Him. You acknowledge you cannot put your hope in your works or performance. You choose to accept His forgiveness and not return to your old ways. Turning at this point, you embark on a journey beyond anything you could ever have dreamed of, free from guilt and death, and alive in Christ!

Now, who are you? Where are you headed?

James 1:26-27

"If anyone thinks himself to be religious, and yet does not bridle his tongue but deceives his own heart, this man's religion is worthless. Pure and undefiled religion in the sight of our God and Father is this to visit orphans and widows in their distress, and to keep oneself unstained by the world."

Have you ever been corrected in a way that seems harsh? How about what James tells us here? If you think you're a devoted Christian, but don't control your words or language, your devotion is worthless. And did you notice that the words James uses here are "does not bridle," as opposed to *cannot* bridle? While everyone slips up once in a while, controlling our words and language is a willful decision we should make and practice as Christians and examples of Jesus to those around us. We *can* control our words and attitudes. Quick to listen, slow to speak, right?

Some people just "don't have a filter." They should get one. They are readily available for the asking. Simply read the Lord's Manual and apply what it says.

What comes out of our mouths indicates what fills our hearts and minds. In Mark 7:1-23, the Lord Jesus makes a distinction between the Pharisees' religious tradition on the one hand, and worshipping in spirit and truth on the other, and points out where our priorities should lie. Jesus, timeless God in human form, repeated in Mark (also recorded in Matthew 23) what he said in Isaiah 1 and the Psalm 51. The Pharisees had lost the true meaning of worship, which God described in Isaiah 1. God was (and still is) sick of meaningless sacrifices and ritualistic worship services at both the church level and at the personal level. What God longs for is a humble heart that earnestly wants to worship in spirit and truth (Micah 6:8)! If you think that you are pleasing God by mouthing songs and prayers that you don't mean, serving on committees so you appear spiritual, or participating in functions so you will be part of the right group, you are deceiving yourself and possibly a few others, but not God. It makes him sick. Your religion, your "devotion," is worthless. Your motivation is coming from your pride and arrogance.

Like bad words defile a person (Mark 7:15), so do bad acts. What you do often reflects what is inside your heart. The opposite is also true—as truthful and healing words bring respect to a man and blessing to God, so do acts of mercy and love. These acts of worship glorify God and build your faith. Giving food and a kind word to someone is worshipping God! Sharing the Gospel and giving hope to the hopeless is worshipping God! Visiting those in retirement homes is worshipping God! Sometimes worshipping God can be hard work, but it's always worth it.

In John 17:14-21, Jesus prays for us, His followers, because we are not part of this world, but we are in it. We are sanctified, set apart, by the word of Truth and Jesus asks that His followers may all be of one heart as He and God are, so that the world may know that Jesus was sent by God. As James says, pure and undefiled religion, worshipping God, is to serve God from a pure heart without selfish motives, thereby keeping ourselves unstained from worldly attitudes and ways.

James 2:1-9

"My brethren, do not hold your faith in our glorious Lord Jesus Christ with an attitude of personal favoritism. For if a man comes into your assembly with a gold ring and dressed in fine clothes, and there also comes in a poor man in dirty clothes, and you pay special attention to the one who is wearing the fine clothes and say "You sit here in a good place," and you say to the poor man "You stand over there, or sit down by my footstool," have you not made distinctions among yourselves, and become judges with evil motives? Listen, my beloved brethren, did not God choose the poor of this world to be rich in faith and heirs of the kingdom which He promised to those who love Him? "But you have dishonored the poor man. Is it not the rich who oppress you and personally drag you into court? Do they not blaspheme the fair name by which you have been called? If, however, you are fulfilling the royal law according to the Scripture, "You shall love your neighbor as yourself," you are doing well. But if you are showing partiality, you are committing sin and are convicted by the law as transgressors."

Am I friendlier, or do I show more partiality in some way, to attractive people? To the wealthy? Or do I show less respect to the wealthy and more to the poor? Am I friendlier toward Christians than to people of other faiths? Every time I judge someone or make a judgement regarding them (sometimes I call it simply "forming an opinion" or an "evaluation," but it's really a judgement) I need a standard to base my judgement on. What is my standard? It's myself. We all have standards that we expect people to live up to, and if they don't then, by default, we place them at some lower level than ourselves. It's our nature, our sin nature.

I have been the victim of prejudice, and I have shown prejudice toward others regarding their race, sex, sexual preference, political party, religion, tattoos and piercings, grammar, handshake, and probably more.

In Leviticus 19:18, the Lord, through Moses, tells His people to not take revenge or hold a grudge against anyone, but to "love your neighbor as yourself." As followers of Christ, we are to love our neighbors in the same way or to the same extent as we love ourselves. It would be difficult for us to prove this godly and brotherly love we profess to have, if in our arrogance, we consider ourselves to be above others or if we begrudge them because they have more than we do. While James' passage specifically mentions material wealth (gold rings or fine clothes), we also make distinctions based on those things I mentioned above – race, politics, sexual preference, and the like. As followers of Jesus, our job is to love people into the Kingdom of God, to show them the same merciful love that Jesus showed and continues to show to us, and to worship God together with them as one family of equals (Galatians 3:28).

We would do well to remember the lesson Jesus spoke of in Matthew 25:34-45. If we have ministered to "the least of these brothers" of Jesus, we have ministered to the Lord Jesus himself.

And tell me who decides who "the *least* of these brothers of mine" are, because He makes no distinction between those brothers (within the church and those without faith) and us. Let us keep our eyes parallel with God's. He sees a person's heart, not the label on their clothes. Rich or poor, we are all equal, and we have all sinned. We have all fallen short of the glory of God (Romans 3:23).

James 2:10-13

"For whoever keeps the whole law and yet stumbles in one point, he has become guilty of all. For He who said, "Do not commit adultery," also said, "Do not commit murder." Now if you do not commit adultery, but do commit murder, you have become a transgressor of the law. So speak and act as those who are to be judged by the law of liberty. For judgment will be merciless to one who has shown no mercy; mercy triumphs over judgment."

In God's economy, we are either sinful or sinless. There are no little white lies. There are no sins that are bigger or worse than others. We are either guilty or guiltless. The sins of Adolf Hitler and Charles Manson are no worse than ours. If we think that we aren't as bad as Hitler or Manson we have proven this verse to be true even within ourselves. I may never have murdered anyone, but if I commit adultery, I'm still guilty. If I have ever told a lie, I'm guilty. The issue is the sin that lives within all of us and how we use it to justify our judgements of others— "the least of these brothers of mine."

Jesus, the physical expression of God's love in action, proved the mercy of God toward us all. But at the final day of God's righteous judgement, there will be no mercy shown to those who showed none themselves. If we love-by-action the people around us, without regard to race, faith, or anything else, we will be living our lives in a manner worthy of our calling. Ephesians 4:1 entreats us to "walk in a manner worthy of our calling," and the rest of the chapter tells us how and why to do that. We are to conduct our lives in a manner that is worthy of the name "Christian," which means, "one like Christ," or "little Christ." We are to live our lives in a way that brings glory and praise to Jesus, not to ourselves. We cannot live a life that brings praise to the Lord when we use our own sinful standards to justify our judgements of others. We are saved by His grace, His mercy, and not by our works, or our performance; this is God's "law of liberty."

The phrase "law of liberty" might sound like an oxymoron, so let's look at what this means. Like our human laws, God's laws declare how things are and how they must be done. Romans 8:1-2 exemplifies "the law of the Spirit of life" (notice the capital *S*). Because of our faith, because of His promise to redeem us, because we are new creations in Christ, and because of Jesus' death and resurrection, there is no condemnation facing us! We are free from the law of sin and death! This is how God views His people, regardless of what our feelings tell us. Our motivation to serve God should be founded firmly in love because of what He did for us, not out of a feeling of guilt, fear, or a need to repay Him (Galatians 5:1,13).

Our salvation through God's mercy is not based on our works, so the mercy we show others should not be based on their works. We cannot earn God's merciful salvation, and we do not deserve it. Unrighteous sinners cannot produce righteous fruit (Matthew 7:16-23; John 15:5). It is only because of His intense and eternal love for us that He provided His son as a sacrifice for our sins (Romans 5:8) and it is only through His son Jesus that we can approach God and ask for forgiveness, or wisdom, or mercy, or anything else. Our ability to show mercy, or to love people around us is a gift from God and is evidence of the presence of His Spirit within us. The desire to show that mercy to others is simply a response to the mercy He showed us (Matthew 5:44-45, Romans 5-6).

James 2:14

"What use is it, my brethren, if a man says he has faith, but he has no works? Can that faith save him?"

Sadly, there are many people who say they are Christians, but have never had a personal relationship with Jesus. It seems that their idea of being "Christian" is to be politically conservative. I know faithful believers "on the other side of the aisle" who could easily dispute that notion.

Faith results from a conviction within a person, brought only by the Holy Spirit, that the Gospel is *Truth*. This conviction is a strong persuasion that causes a change of mind, a change in the way a person thinks and reasons. We cannot produce this type of faith ourselves. Because of our sin nature we have no desire to. Prior to coming to this type of faith we may believe in God, and we may go to church, but these practices in themselves cannot change our hearts (2 Corinthians 4:16-18; Ephesians 3:16-19). Until God, through the Holy Spirit and through the Gospel (Romans 10:17), convicts us of our sin and shows us our need for redemption, we cannot produce the righteousness required by Him. Hebrews 11:6-7 says Noah, like us, "became an heir of the righteousness" by faith, and that it is impossible to please God without faith.

According to Hebrews 12:2, Jesus is the author and finisher, or completer, of our faith and that faith is the foundation of our hope. Hebrews 11:1 (King James version) says, "Faith is the *substance* of things hoped for, and the evidence of things not seen." While faith itself is invisible, when we see people standing firm in their conviction that the Gospel is Truth, their actions, words, and lifestyles that glorify God makes their faith visible. The presence of this type of faith is evidenced by traits like inner stability, security within themselves because of the presence of the Holy Spirit, and firmness in that they are not easily swayed. Such people of faith are trustworthy and show constancy over a long period of time and through trials. It is complete and total reliance upon God.

If I said that I loved my wife, but never did anything that showed it, how could she or anyone else believe it to be true? Without the visible proof of my actions, I cannot prove my love for her exists. If I don't hold her hand as we walk, if I don't give her flowers or send her a romantic card, if I don't care for her when she is sick, pray for her, or kiss her in public, how is anyone going to know I love her? How would *she* know? Perhaps more importantly, if I completely ignore her or abuse her privately but make myself appear to be the doting husband in public, there is something seriously wrong with my reasoning. The only person being fooled is myself.

The same principle is true regarding a relationship with Jesus. If I seldom or never read my Bible, if I seldom or never pray, if I don't tithe, if I don't spend time around other Christians, if my habits or lifestyle haven't changed, if church is not important to me, if I haven't shared the Gospel with anyone, how am I really any different than I was before I said I became a Christian? Even though my faith is not dependent on my actions, it is expressed by them. Faith is the system of the Gospel truth itself; it's how the Gospel works. It is how a formerly sinful person can have peace with a Holy God. It is how we can still have joy while enduring terrible pain (James 1:2; Hebrews 13:5).

Having said all that, any honest believer will tell you that there have been times when their faith has been weak, maybe even absent. We do things we know we shouldn't do, and don't do the things we know we should be doing. Does this mean the Spirit has left us? Does it mean we aren't saved any more, or that God has given up on us? Absolutely not. Romans 7 addresses the battle between the sinful nature that is within us and the desire to do the will of God. Only clinging to Jesus by faith frees us from sin's grasp.

James 2:15-18

"If a brother or sister is without clothing and in need of daily food, and one of you says to them, 'Go in peace, be warmed and be filled,' and yet you do not give them what is necessary for their body, what use is that? Even so faith, if it has no works, is dead, being by itself. But someone may well say, "You have faith, and I have works; show me your faith without the works, and I will show you my faith by my works."

Long ago, a Bible instructor told me that the only thing a person really needs to make the decision to repent of their sins and follow Jesus is the Gospel. This is true, but if that person is too hungry to think and too cold to follow anybody anywhere, then what we need to do is meet that brother's or sister's physical needs and then minister to their spiritual needs. We need to be sure that cold and hungry brother or sister understands that the food, blanket, and shelter come from Jesus because He loves them with a sacrificial love and wants to give them so much more! They must see His love, power, and presence in the lives and actions of the people giving the food, blankets, and shelter. They must see that above all else. This is what James' discussion of works is all about—showing a dying, hurting world that change can happen, and it comes through the love of Jesus flowing through His people on the street, in a tomato field, in a forest—anywhere. If it happens at a church building, wonderful! But it can happen anywhere God's people are together and united.

Is it only the cold, hungry, or homeless that need to be ministered to? Everyone has needs. Everyone needs to know someone else genuinely cares for them. What about the Wall Street executive, the police officer, the white supremacist, the neighbor next door, your wife, your husband, your kids? They all need to hear the Gospel. You can't simply tell them your life is different now. They need to see a change in you—perhaps in the way you do business, how you react when angered, or in your priorities. Your actions will speak for you much louder and clearer than your words alone.

Your motivations for doing what you do are important. Are you doing these "good works" just to score points with God? That is a bad idea and a waste of time. We've already discussed that God doesn't owe anyone anything, ever. Are you doing them to look good to other people? Matthew 6:5-16 addresses this regarding prayer and fasting, but the same principle is true regarding looking for the praise or recognition of people rather than God. Remember the story of Jesus riding into Jerusalem on a donkey in Matthew 2:6-11? One minute the people are cheering and the next they're yelling for Him to be crucified. Don't let your works be motivated by the praise of the people; they may turn on you when you need them most. Work for the praise of God, who loves you no matter what.

James 2:19-24

"You believe that God is one. You do well; the demons also believe, and shudder. But are you willing to recognize, you foolish fellow, that faith without works is useless? "Was not Abraham our father justified by works when he offered up Isaac his son on the altar? You see that faith was working with his works, and as a result of the works, faith was perfected; and the Scripture was fulfilled which says, "And Abraham believed God, and it was reckoned to him as righteousness," and he was called the friend of God. You see that a man is justified by works and not by faith alone."

At the beginning of this study, I said that what you believe regarding who God is and the strength of that belief will greatly influence how you serve God. James points out that belief is not the only determiner of how you serve God. James says if you believe in one God, that's a great start, but that the demons believe the same thing you do. They shudder at the thought of God because they were once in the presence of the one true living God. They have seen His glory and realize His infinite power and authority. Demons believe in God and acknowledge His power, but refuse to acknowledge His authority, so they are condemned to Hell. They were in Heaven and were removed in their rebellion with Satan (Isaiah 14:15; Ezekiel 28:16-17).

As I look around this country and the world, I think people ought to consider what can be learned from the demons not submitting to God's authority. Many people can't decide if the god they believe in is their heavenly father, or mother, or an "it." But even for those who have settled on the God of the Bible, believing *in* Him is not enough. Believing there is one God who created everything, who is all-powerful, full of mercy, and loves all of us is good and true, but simply claiming this belief is not how God asks us to live our lives.

James asks if we are willing to recognize that faith without works is useless. If your professed faith does not cause you to want to change the way you run your life, it's pointless. Why even say you believe? It's empty talk. Christianity is not passive, and neither should we who profess Jesus as Lord be passive (Matthew 7:21, 24-25; John 9:31). We should wait on the Lord as we would wait on tables if we worked in a restaurant. We should be moving, working, and serving. When we do not act in faith, we are saying that we do not trust God enough to do what He has asked us. When we do not trust Him, we cannot experience His mighty work through us; we cannot be a part of the powerful things He does. Do we always want to simply sit on the sidelines as others are being blessed by Him because of their obedience, because they trusted Him enough to serve others? I don't think so. Talk is cheap. Make your actions testify to your faith (look back to James 2:18).

James illustrates his argument that faith cannot exist without actions by going back to Abraham, the founder of the Jewish (and therefore Christian) faith.In Genesis 22:1-14, God doesn't ask, but tells Abraham to take his only son Isaac, whom he loved to a certain place and offer him as a burnt offering. With two servants and his son, Abraham chopped wood for the offering then travelled three days to the place God told them to go. What was Abraham thinking as they walked, as he watched his son eat dinner by a campfire, as he laid down to sleep at night? When they reached the place, Abraham told the men to wait. "The boy and I will go over there, worship, and be right back." While walking, Isaac asked, "Dad, we have the wood and the knife, but where's the lamb?" Abraham responded, "God will provide."

I'm intrigued by the fact that there is no conversation recorded between father and son as Abraham builds the alter and arranges the wood on it, or as he ties up his son, or as he puts Isaac on the wood and raises the knife to kill him. Emotionally, I would be torn to shreds! Is it possible to willingly obey God while also feeling deeply sad about what it is God has told you to do? Surely, there must have been eye-contact between them at some time. During this process there were many opportunities for Abraham to stop and say, "I can't do this!" But Abraham believed God. He believed God's promise that he would have decedents through Isaac (Genesis 21:12). However, Abraham did not know what would be required of him in the meantime. We've been given promises by God also; do we really want to know what the future will bring, what we will go through to receive His promises? Isn't it better to simply trust God?

As we go through life, there will be many opportunities for us to bail out of hard situations with our family and friends as we do things that God has led us to do. At times we seem to reach a point of obedience that we cannot cross. God is asking too much. But this is the point where His purifying fire burns, and faith and friendship are forged. This is where the dross of selfishness hisses away and strength of heart is perfected. If we bail at the last minute, all the pain we have gone through has been wasted; all that's left is a scar and every time we see it, we will remember what we almost achieved.

As Abraham began to bring the knife down toward Isaac, the angel of the Lord (many believe this is Jesus) stopped him, saying, "Now I know that you fear God." Abraham's obedience, based on growing faith, showed that he trusted in God. Abraham demonstrated his faith in God by doing what God commanded him. Abraham looked beyond the heartrending command to the promise that God had given him regarding Isaac (Genesis 21:12). By his actions Abraham was, indeed, justifying his claim to be a follower of God. James 2:23 says Abraham *believed God,* and he was counted as righteous. The verse does not say Abraham believed *in* God. As a result, James tells us, God called Abraham His friend. This was not blind faith, but vision through faith.

How would you feel to know beyond doubt that the omnipotent, eternal Lord God thought of you as His friend? Did you know that you *can* have this sure knowledge? In John 15:14-15 Jesus calls those who obey his commands his friends.

I know that greater things are both required and accomplished between two brothers who have committed to each other in a friendship that has been through fire than between brothers who think the fire is none of their business or is beyond what they're comfortable with. Friends may have to confront one another about a drinking problem, about an affair, about their walks with God. Good friends can be trusted and will know when the issue is more than a simple difference of opinion or mistaken perception. Like Jesus, good friends, solid friends, brothers or sisters in the Lord, will go with you through the fire and will not abandon you in hard and trying times. I have friends like this, who have gone through some pretty ugly times with me; they do the work of God, and I thank God for them.

Has God asked me to do some hard things? Sure. Was I faithful in all of them? No, but I try, and just as importantly I look beyond my failures or weaknesses to the promise that He gave to me—that He will never give up on me and I will, one day, be with Him in Heaven.

A faith without works is, indeed, dead, lifeless. But a life lived by faith is new and alive every day.

Oh, what a friend we have in Jesus!

James 2:25-26

"And in the same way was not Rahab the harlot also justified by works when she received the messengers and sent them out another way? For just as the body without the spirit is dead, so also faith without works is dead."

Sometimes, when we react to a situation we hadn't planned for, our actions bring out a depth of conviction that perhaps we weren't aware of—we "go with our gut." Sometimes, our need to do the right thing right now exceeds what might be socially correct. Such was the situation for Rahab.

In chapter 2 of Joshua, the two spies Joshua sent into the land found lodging in the house of a Gentile (non-Jew) prostitute named Rahab. Somehow the presence of the spies was reported to the king, and he immediately sent his men to find the spies at her house. Rahab sent all the king's men away saying, "Yes, they were here, but I didn't know where they were from and when it was time to close the gate they went out. If you hurry, you can catch them." A Gentile prostitute protected some Jewish invaders by deceiving government officials. Why? Because she, and the people of the land, had heard what the Lord was doing and how other cities were completely destroyed by God's people. Rahab said, "Our hearts melted and no courage remained in any man any longer because of you; for the Lord your God, He is God in heaven above, and on earth beneath" (Joshua 2:11). She let the men down through a window in the wall with their promise that she and her family would be saved from destruction. When the Israelites defeated her city, they protected Rahab's family and integrated them into the people of Israel. Rahab married an Israelite man, and Rahab, a Gentile prostitute, became part of the lineage of David, and therefore, the lineage of Jesus.

Rahab realized that the God of Israel was more powerful than the gods worshipped in Jericho. She found her religious priorities were all wrong, and that the only reasonable thing to do was to put herself and her family at the mercy of the spies who represented the God who completely destroyed cities. She put herself and her family in a very precarious position. She double-crossed her own people and relied on the integrity of the spies and the mercy of God. Somehow Rahab recognized that

God—despite His heavy hand against those who opposed Him and His people—would show mercy to those who put their faith in Him into action.

If a harlot today heard the Gospel, realized who Jesus is, repented, and then walked into a church service, would the mercy of God through the integrity of His people be evident to her? Would she see integrity between our words and our actions? Rahab's convictions led her to act on what she knew to be right, and as a result of her trust and obedience she and her family were saved.

James 2:26 says just as our physical bodies need the spirit to live, so our faith needs works to live. Your physical body needs work, it needs exercise to be healthy. Your faith needs work and exercise also. People who are active live longer and have happier lives. And you know that if you leave a potato sitting on a couch long enough it will rot. Recall our discussion regarding James 1:3-4—your faith, your trust, and your confidence in Jesus (and therefore, your attitude toward life and your joy) will be so much stronger and healthier if you trust your Trainer and do what He says.

James 3:1

"Let not many of you become teachers, my brethren, knowing that as such we shall incur a stricter judgement."

If you think you want to become a teacher, first realize that you will be held to a stricter judgement.

James is addressing reasons or motivations of people wanting to teach, not the gift they may have for teaching. But why a stricter judgement?

First, any pride or vanity we have within us can be easily fed by teaching others. It makes us feel good when we can teach someone how something works, what something means, or why something is right or wrong. But if we're not careful to check our pride along the way, we may soon become arrogant, regardless of how much we know or what gift we may have. Everyone, like it or not, teaches somebody something, whether we are showing someone how to weld, balance a checkbook, or learn something in the Bible. We can be teachers even when simply having a conversation. All of us are influencers. All of us have the power to influence someone for good or bad. According to 2 Corinthians 5:20, all Christians are ambassadors for Jesus to the world. Ambassadors are teachers in a way, teaching foreign countries about the countries they represent. Since all believers are in the position of teachers and ambassadors, we must all bring the same, uniform, coherent message to the world. While we may bring it with differing methods or ministries, or into different environments, the Gospel must remain the same. There is only one Truth, one Gospel, and all believers need to seek a solid understanding of this one Gospel. We cannot shrug off responsibility as influencers to share Jesus with the world simply because we are not pastors or ministers or church staff members.

Secondly, biblical teachers are the architects of the church of the future. Think of the analogy of tossing a stone into a pond and the ripples that causes. What one person teaches now may be multiplied and taught to many in the future. In other words, what is taught now will shape what future generations learn. It is then no wonder that James cautions against too many people becoming teachers. Believers considering becoming teachers should investigate their motives and fill this consideration with prayer. The need for Spirit-filled teachers (in the church especially, but also in schools) is enormous. Teaching is a profession and a ministry with tremendous rewards but also comes with challenges. With any great position comes great responsibility so biblical teachers must be vigilant regarding what they teach. They themselves must submit to Biblical teaching from mature Christians. They must carefully study Scripture themselves. They must constantly seek God's Spirit regarding the material. And they must remember that they will be held accountable for what they have taught. Paul, in Galatians 1:6-10, has strong words for anyone who would teach another "gospel" message: "Let him be accursed."

In 1985 I became a father for the first time. The second time was fourteen months later in 1987. Now I am also the grandfather of three very fine young people. As a parent and grandparent, I am responsible for teaching my children and grandchildren, preparing them for how to deal with what life throws at them as they enter the world. I am being watched constantly by them. What I teach them, or more correctly, what they learn from me (there is a difference), will influence how they relate to others, how they relate to Jesus and, to some extent, how others relate to them. The lessons they learn from me will impact how they run their businesses and how they serve their families. They will hear in my words and see in my actions what I believe, and whatever they hear or see most often is what they will regard as acceptable behavior. My beliefs will also become part of the foundation of their theology. This is a sobering thought for me. In essence, we parents are creating the moral and spiritual root stock for the church of the future.

I think it's interesting that this section addressing teachers follows James' discussion regarding our tongue. Our tongue is the best exemplar of what fills our hearts. It is the proof of whether the re-born person is in action, or if our own selfish will is still in control. When people are walking through life in close friendship with Jesus with the Holy Spirit guiding them, knowledge and wisdom will be evident in more than just their words; it will be seen in their lifestyle. Those who witness this and hear their words will learn about the Gospel. Think about this: what is one of the biggest arguments against Christianity? The hypocrisy the world sees in Christians. To a large extent they have a good argument—we Christians have been pretty self-righteous at times. Some of our teaching has been, well, less than Spirit-filled. Our lifestyles, our words, our testimonies must be evidence of the fruit of the Spirit (Galatians 5:22).

James 3:2-4

"For we all stumble in many ways. If anyone does not stumble in what he says, he is a perfect man, able to bridle the whole body as well. Now if we put bits into the horses' mouths so that they may obey us, we direct their entire body as well. Behold, the ships also, though they are so great and are driven by strong winds, are still directed by a very small rudder, wherever the inclination of the pilot desires."

When James writes about the striking responsibility teachers have, it might seem as though only perfect people should be teachers. But if it were so, there would be no teachers because nobody's perfect, right? So many churches have split because of differences of opinion as to what should be taught. We teach what we believe, so splits happen when the church is in confusion as to what it believes. The church still gets upset because the world doesn't understand our message. Have we understood our own message?

What James says in verse 2 is that people who do not stumble (sin) in what they say or how they say it can control the rest of their bodies in a sinless manner as well because our words are tools that direct our hearts. Jesus was the only person to keep His tongue, His communication, and His words in control at all times. Controlling our speech isn't limited to curbing profanity, but also refers to refraining from interrupting people, speaking truth at the right time and with the right tone, and deciding if you really need to speak at all in a given moment. We as a culture spend too much time in health clubs and diet centers trying to get our bodies under control when we should be putting more sweat into getting our words and language under control. What if putting energy into disciplining your tongue was the key to learning to discipline your body?

Horses need to be controlled by a person if they are to do any kind of constructive work. They cannot plow or perform completely alone, even if trained, because they have neither the desire nor the understanding to accomplish the task their master asks them to do. We are the same way. We have neither the desire nor the ability to control our tongues apart from the Holy Spirit (John 5:30, 15:5). We must yield ourselves to His direction in order for anything good to come out of our lives. Controlling our speech to honor God is one way of yielding to Him.

Have you ever found yourself promising to do something you never really wanted to follow through with? You let your tongue take you somewhere you really didn't want to go. Our culture is a strong wind trying to pull us in every direction it thinks is important at the time, and we have to struggle against the winds and contend with the current to keep from being blown off course. To remain on course is our duty. To remain on course is a decision we make to follow the Pilot of our souls, who knows where the rocks and the shallows are and who understands the tides of the world. The crew of a ship trusts their captain to direct them in the best way to their destination. Even if we think we know better than the Pilot (which we don't), we need to relinquish our control to Him if we expect to reach those peaceful shores. If we don't know our Pilot, if we don't obey the Holy Spirit, we become like a ship without a rudder, adrift and at the "mercy" of the storm—and there is no mercy in a storm.

James uses "the tongue" to refer to the words we say aloud, but it doesn't take much imagination to extend his points to the words that remain unsaid in our heads—the words we say to ourselves and the attitudes that fill our hearts. Our tongues express our thoughts, but although the words we speak to ourselves may never be heard, they nonetheless direct our lives like the horse's bit or the ship's rudder. When we don't listen to the Holy Spirit, one of the consequences is that we start listening to lies.

Nazi leader Joseph Goebbels said if you tell a person the same lie enough times, they will, in time, believe it as fact. Unfortunately, Goebbels knew all too well what he was talking about. He had contributed to feeding thousands of German people repeated lies about the Jews and had seen those lies transform the mindset of Nazi Germany. In the same way, if a child grows up constantly being told she is fat, stupid, mediocre, or worthless, she will grow up believing she is exactly that. As people think they are, so they are. On the other hand, if a child is told she is loved, important, creative, and that she matters to those around her, she will grow up believing she is exactly that. As people think they are, so they are.

Where does your tongue lead you? What do your spoken and unspoken words tell you about your identity? Do they tell you that as a follower of Jesus, you are a child of God, heir of His grace, created in His image, the bride of Christ chosen by Him?

In Romans 12, Paul urges us to present ourselves to God and not be conformed any longer to the world's system. He tells us to be transformed through the renewing of our minds. His words hold true regarding not only our service to God, but also the way we think about ourselves. If, as a follower of Christ, I see myself as a don't-call-me-I-got-no-talent, go-to-church-and-leave wallflower, and I do nothing with the talents Jesus has given me, how is Jesus going to be glorified, and how am I going to bear any fruit (Matthew 25:24-25)?

Believe what Scripture says about you! As a follower of Jesus, you are a new creation, created in His image with God-given gifts and talents that the Holy Spirit uses through you to glorify God! Refuse to use any part of your body to fulfill your lusts of the flesh. Use your tongue (your words), to encourage others, to share the Gospel, to bring hope to a dark world! Do not listen to others if they insult you about anything; you are a child of the resurrected King of Kings, an heir of grace, so listen to Him! Because He created you, He knows exactly what you are capable of. He has confidence in you. Have the same confidence in Him.

James 3:5-8

"So also, the tongue is a small part of the body, and yet it boasts of great things. Behold, how great a forest fire is set aflame by such a small fire! And the tongue is a fire, the very world of iniquity; the tongue is set among the members as that which defiles the entire body, and sets on fire the course of your life, and is set on fire by hell. For every species of beasts and birds, or reptiles and creatures of the sea, is tamed, and has been tamed by the human race. But no one can tame the tongue; it is a restless evil and full of deadly poison."

When we talk about our "tongues," we're describing our attitudes, the words we choose, and our body language, all of which show the listener a polaroid picture of what really resides within us. Too often, when we speak of how we use our tongues, we narrow the conversation to be about angry outbursts, but that's not the only case. It also could include continual humor at another person's expense. It could be teasing, smooth and sensual. It could be habitual lying, gossiping, cussing, constantly interrupting, or slander. I'm sure there are others, but these are all expressions of what is living inside us. In Matthew 15:11, Jesus says, "It's what comes *out* of a man's mouth that defiles him." In Luke 6:45 (CEV), he says, "Good people do good things because of the good in their hearts, but bad people do bad things because of the evil in their hearts. Your words show what is in your heart." Essentially, our speech reveals what is already in our hearts. If we truly believe Scripture, the implications here are monumental.

Without discipline, our tongues can destroy the course of our lives. James tells us our tongues are set afire through the influences of the spirits from hell, full of deadly poison.

Is it any wonder that James says that no person can tame the tongue? He emphasizes the importance of abiding in Christ or taking root in Christ (John 15) and the renewing of your mind, allowing God to change the way you think (Romans 12:2). If what comes out of us is what defiles us, then our inner selves, our hearts, the deepest parts of us, that which is set afire by the spirits from hell, must be made clean and the deadly poison removed. We might be able to clean up our appearance, but only repentance and the Holy Spirit can clean the inside of a person and remove the poison. How does this change happen? Through the power of the Holy Spirit.

In Ephesians 3:14-19, Paul prays for believers this way:

"[I pray] that He would grant you, according to the riches of His glory, to be strengthened with power through His Spirit in the inner man, so that Christ may dwell in your hearts through faith; and that you, being rooted and grounded in love, may be able to comprehend with all the saints what is the breadth and length and height and depth, and to know the love of Christ which surpasses knowledge, that you may be filled up to all the fullness of God."

If Christ dwells in our hearts through faith, and we are grounded in love and have experienced for ourselves the love of Christ so that we are filled up to all the fullness of God, then there will be no room, no allowance, for the spirits of Hell in us. What a wonderful prayer to pray for each other! God, give us the ability to think before we speak.

James 3:9-12

"With it we bless our Lord and Father, and with it we curse men, who have been made in the likeness of God; from the same mouth come both blessing and cursing. My brethren, these things ought not to be this way. Does a fountain send out from the same opening both fresh and bitter water? Can a fig tree, my brethren, produce olives, or a vine produce figs? Nor can salt water produce fresh."

For the ancient Hebrews, a word spoken was not just a sound on the lips, but an agent sent out from the soul. So, a curse was an active agent sent out from one person's soul for the purpose of hurting another. This is interesting when you think back to Matthew 15:11, when Jesus says that it is what comes out of a man that defiles him. Behind the word spoken stands the soul that created it. Consider what this means as you study the Word of God as a whole, the words of Jesus as you read them, and the power of the words you pray. How should this affect how we pray and speak? Do the words in Scripture impact us differently now as we consider them as active agents sent out from God?

It is so important to realize the power of words. Maybe it would do us moderns good to adopt the Hebrew attitude toward words and language—agents sent out from the soul. We take language far too lightly. One minute we're singing praise songs and blessing the Lord, and the next we're calling somebody a jerk, or worse. Words can be the balm that heals, warm rays of hope and encouragement, a loving rod of correction, or the sword and chain of rudeness, slander, and murder. The choice is ours. Let the agent sent out reflect a reborn soul.

Back in verse two James said *Hey, we all stumble at times, only a perfect person doesn't stumble.* We all say things that we didn't intend to, so don't point fingers at someone because they tripped over a word or two. So often we allow a few words to offend us and give us an excuse to stop listening to the rest of the statement. Within the past few years, both Christians and non-Christians have greatly increased their use of their "right to free speech." First, I believe that no speech is "free"—there is profit or loss, benefit or hurt, in everything said. Second, even though we have this right to "free speech," we should not take our freedom as license to verbalize or act out whatever is rattling around in our minds, especially in emotionally heated moments. Since we're talking about controlling our tongues, I hesitate to use the word "fool," but the book of Proverbs does, so I'm going with it. Proverbs 26:4 says, "Do not answer a fool according to his folly, unless you be like him yourself." Proverbs 14:7 says, "Leave a foolish argument, because you will not find words of knowledge." And Proverbs 13:6 says, "Every prudent man acts with knowledge, but a fool flaunts his folly."

Let's consider one more thing. When a born-again Christian does, for instance, slander a brother, Satan will jump at the chance to accuse both the slanderer and the victim of not really being saved. *You're not a good Christian! You think you're saved? Joe is a Christian and he doesn't talk like you! You're just the same as you always have been!*

Don't believe these lies. If you can remember giving your life to Jesus, confessing Him as Lord, confessing your sins, and thereby being cleansed by His blood and by faith at some point in time, then you are born again, a new creation, sealed by the Holy Spirit for the day of redemption (Ephesians 4:30), an heir of God's grace and loved by Him. Our salvation is not dependent on what we have done or can do. None of us on our own will ever be good enough to get into Heaven. Our salvation and our deliverance from the power of death is based on what Jesus did on the cross and through His resurrection, not our performance (John 19:30 and Romans 7:14-25).

Slander, division, character assassination... Oh, brothers, things ought not to be this way, but sadly they often are. However, the freedom we have in Jesus sets us free from the herd mentality of the world. Colossians 3:1 tells us, "If you have been raised with Christ, set your mind on things above, where Christ is, seated at the right hand of God." Likewise, Romans 8:5 says, "For those who live according to the flesh set their minds on the things of the flesh, but those who live according to the Spirit set their minds on the things of the Spirit." If we set our minds on the things of the Spirit of God, we will be a spring of refreshing, cool, clean water to a world that is dying of thirst.

James 3:13-18

"Who among you is wise and understanding? Let him show by his good behavior his deeds in the gentleness of wisdom. But if you have bitter jealousy and selfish ambition in your heart, do not be arrogant and so lie against the truth. This wisdom is not that which comes down from above, but is earthly, natural, demonic. For where jealousy and selfish ambition exist, there is disorder and every evil thing. But the wisdom from above is first pure, then peaceable, gentle, reasonable, full of mercy and good fruits, unwavering, without hypocrisy. And the seed whose fruit is righteousness is sown in peace by those who make peace."

The golden rule for polite conversation has been to never discuss finances, politics, or religion. It's easy to see how comparing paychecks or political candidates could get dicey, but what about religion? Why can't we talk about religion in everyday conversation? I think it's because the conversation can only have one possible rational conclusion if carried out long enough: that the sinfulness of all humanity creates the need for a hero, a deliverer, a savior, and that savior is Jesus Christ alone. But then, for some, putting their hope for eternal life in somebody who lived and died 2,000 years ago doesn't seem like wisdom; and people have a lot of barriers they put up between themselves and belief, some for good reason. The wisdom of this world and the wisdom from above clash with a terrible noise. But, what's the difference between the world's wisdom and that wisdom from above?

Proverbs 1:7 tells us, "The fear [the adoration, worship] of the Lord is the beginning of knowledge; fools despise wisdom and instruction." To realize who God is and who you are in relation to Him is the beginning of wisdom. God is Holy; you are not. God is the Creator, Sustainer, and Center of all existence; you are not. There are many brilliant people in the world who know a lot of stuff and pride themselves in their wisdom regarding that stuff, but they have no knowledge or understanding of their Creator. Many are unable or unwilling to acknowledge His existence. Their words may sound impressive, but James has just told us how the tongue can make great boasts while paving the pathway to destruction. Anyone can say they have wisdom, but true, godly wisdom that gives insight and understanding into things of the world and God himself comes only out of a relationship with God through Jesus. The proof of wisdom, whether worldly or godly, lies in our actions.

One of the adjectives James uses in describing godly wisdom is "reasonable." This word means "willing to yield." There is a time when the reasonable thing, the smart thing, the sensible thing to do is to yield, to set aside the plans and goals we have forged in stone for ourselves and explore the possibility that the Gospel is true. Believing that God exists is one of the foundations for faith (Hebrews 11:6). One day, all people will stand before God, and those who didn't believe He existed will have to give an account of their lives to Him and why they did not acknowledge Him as Lord. What can they possibly say? The universe will echo with silence. What a feeling of utter hopelessness and aloneness. At that point they will realize how foolish their "wisdom" was, and how foolish they were to reject His grace and Truth, but it will be too late.

The fear of the Lord is the beginning of wisdom. Cultivating a friendship with Jesus causes wisdom to grow, and mature wisdom in the form of the moving love of Jesus reaches out to share the Gospel (1 Corinthians 1:18). The "seed" James refers to in verse 18 is the Good News, the Gospel. When the Gospel is shared (or "planted" in another person, to carry the analogy) in peace by those who strive to live peacefully, it can produce righteousness in them (see Matthew 13:19-23).

In Luke 13:19-20, Jesus tells a parable about very small things being used to accomplish very large things—a mustard seed and yeast. The variety of mustard that Jesus is describing here is not like our common mustard. It a very small seed that grows to be a plant as high as twelve feet. When birds build nests, they look for a place that offers shelter and protection. At that time, the Kingdom of God was made up of Jesus and twelve wavering guys who planted the Gospel as they went along. With the Holy Spirit's cultivation, just look at what it has grown into since then: the Christian church world-wide and God's grace within the hearts of believers! In a similar way, it takes only a very small amount of yeast kneaded into the bread dough to make it rise. Never underestimate what you as one follower of Jesus can do. Your one small act of service to Jesus just might bring about some huge things for His glory!

James 4:1-2a

"What is the source of quarrels and conflicts among you? Is it not the source of your pleasures that wage war in your members? You lust and do not have; so, you commit murder. You are envious and cannot obtain; so, you fight and quarrel."

How does pleasure create conflict? At the end of chapter 3, James makes clear the vast contrasts between godly wisdom and the wisdom of the world, demonstrated by the fruit, or the product, of each. He presents these differences in wisdom and then asks the believers there, *So, what's causing your problems? I'll tell you what's causing them, you're not searching for wisdom from above! You have chosen to follow your own worldly wisdom, your own plans, and your own rules, your own desires, and as a result you're fighting and arguing between yourselves within the body of Christ.* The seeds of righteousness are sown in peace (3:18), but there's no peace here, so how can any righteousness be produced?

Think back to James 1:7-8, about the unstable man not getting anything from God, and Matthew 6:21, which says no one can serve two masters. That's what's happening here. Believers are trying to please God while also pursuing self-fulfillment through their own sinful pleasures. We don't know the exact subject of their disagreements, but James' words indicate some pretty serious disagreements. It's no wonder that in verse 4 James calls them "adulteresses." They have left their first love. They say, "Yes, Lord, we love you, but we also love these other things! We believe our ways are the best ways for people to live, and we're willing to wage war against other believers to get there." This is not a godly stance. Either we are doing our best to follow the Holy Spirit's leading, or we still have other priorities. Either we are doing our part to maintain and promote peace and order in the church or we're part of the problem. There's nothing in between. Proverbs 6:16-19 says it is an abomination for someone to spread strife among the brothers.

The "you" in this passage addresses the church as a whole (believers experiencing conflict with other believers) and individuals (Christians experiencing conflict within themselves). When we apply these verses to the individual Christian, we should turn back to Romans 7. Paul describes the conflict that exists within every Christian every day: that of the desire to sin and the desire to do the will of God and abide in Him. Am I going to do what I want to do, or am I going to do what I know the Spirit is leading me to do? Honestly, I think the choice to follow the Lord's leading can be hard to make. If we are honest with ourselves, we would have to agree that sin can be a lot of fun... for a while. It can feel great... for a while. Maybe you even prayed about it, and God didn't actually prevent you from doing it, did He?

Does *all* pleasure create conflict? For instance, does it cause problems to enjoy a day at the lake or go to a car show? Are there issues with shopping for clothes or going to movies? How about volunteering for a church position or committee? It takes two for conflict to happen. In any of these examples, the activity itself is not the issue, it is neither good or bad. The cause of conflict, either within yourself (that is, between yourself and Jesus) or between you and another person (and Jesus), arises from the reasons or priorities behind your desire for the pleasure. Are you going to the lake to enjoy the beauty and peace of God's creation or are you running from responsibilities that you're not facing up to? Do you go to car shows and appreciate the work and art people have put into their projects, or to feed your lust for something you can't have? Do you spend money for clothes and that you need and have budgeted for, or do you put things you don't need on credit cards that you haven't paid off? Are the movies you go to appropriate for you as a follower of Christ? Is your participation in these church committees taking away time you know you should be investing in your family, or is your participation your means for recognition? Does *all* pleasure create conflict? No. The conflict is created when our search for pleasure and self-fulfillment (which is idolatry) overpowers our desire for Jesus.

Whom will you serve? Whom will you yield to? Who knows better, you, or Jesus? We all fail at times. We all stumble in this walk with Jesus. And Satan immediately jumps on our backs, accusing us and pointing to our failures, the same old failures over and over and over. Paul makes it clear that it is no longer you that sins, but it is that sin-nature that lives within you (Romans 7:17). The more we yield ourselves to God and the Holy Spirit, the more we will be able to resist the lies of our enemy Satan. This decision to yield to God does not come from a mind focused on its own pleasures. It comes from one that has been renewed by the Spirit of God, who begins to implant His wisdom from above (Romans 12:1-2, Psalm 119:9-16). Renewed or not, the mind produces thoughts built from what's in our hearts. Thoughts produce actions or words. Actions and words produce an image or reputation that other people will know you by. People will often judge the church they see you come out of on the basis of your behavior. Are you kind and generous? Are you judgmental? Compassionate? Welcoming? If you live your life as much like Jesus as you can, and I do the same, then the Bride of Christ will stand pure and beautifully radiant in an increasingly darkening world with her lamps ready when He comes to collect her home. We are powerful, beautiful, resurrected soldiers of the cross! And we serve the Lord Jesus Christ only.

Do we really commit murder when we lust after someone else's things, or wife, or husband? Well, David literally did in 2 Samuel 11. For the rest of us, however, the murder is usually more subtle. For the sake of self-image, in order to be in seen in the right social or business circles, men and women in the church have sacrificed their families at the altar of wealth and ambition, living beyond their means and getting deeply into debt. They have killed their own reputations and sometimes themselves because they weren't able to achieve what someone else had. Men and women in the church have slandered the characters of other members of the church body for having differing points-of-view, defaming their brother or sister to undermine the validity of the counterargument, attempting to make their own views appear superior. It's no wonder that James strongly cautions us regarding the use of our tongues in chapter 3. If we're a part of this slanderous behavior, how do we have the audacity to approach the throne of grace and wonder why God hasn't answered our prayers like He said He would? (Matthew 7:4-5). In John 13:34 Jesus gives us a new command, to love one another. We can't have Christ-like love for a person and slander him at the same time. Confess your sin to God and He will cleanse you from it (1John 1:9). Go to the other person, confess to them and ask them to forgive you (James 5:16). How good it is to live at peace with each other (Ps.133).

James 4:2b-4

"You do not have because you do not ask. You ask and do not receive, because you ask with many wrong motives, so that you may spend it on your pleasures. You adulteresses, do you not know that friendship with the world is hostility toward God? Therefore, whoever wishes to be a friend of the world makes himself an enemy of God."

James continues by saying, "You don't have because you don't ask." We are loved by God who is limitless in every aspect, who wants us to have abundant life, and we don't ask? Why not? Why don't we ask? Do we think we're not worthy? Worthy of what — asking God for anything? Not worthy of being given what you're asking for? Maybe you think He'll just say no anyway?

Verse 3 brings up another possibility — you ask with the wrong motives, so you can "spend it on your pleasures." *Who said my motives were wrong? Nobody knows why I'm asking for this!* God does. And He loves you so much that He often protects you from ruining your life by not allowing the things you're asking for even if at the time it seems to you that your motives are fine. Our motives are not always wrong or bad. Sometimes we are asking for holy things for holy reasons, and yet we still do not see the fulfillment of what we're asking for. Hebrews 11 lists people who, though asking faithfully for God's promises, waited their whole lives without seeing the fulfillment. In this case, however, James seems to know that the believers he is writing to have fallen into asking for things based on their pleasures, rather than God's pleasures.

After a long period of time not receiving what I am pleading with God for, I often conclude that He, for whatever reason, doesn't want me to have it. Because I trust His judgments, I go with that and move on in my pursuit of Him. At one time I had a friend who was so deeply depressed for so long that I thought the best thing for him was for God to take him home to Heaven. So that's what I prayed for. He was so sad, and I wanted his life to get better. Looking back, I can see now (but not then) the blessing He gave me by denying my request, even as good as I thought my motives were.

After generations of telling His people that the things they were pursuing were bad for them, in grief and anger, He "gave them over" to things that would destroy them in the long run as in Romans 1:24. He said, *Fine. You think you know what is best. You refuse to trust me, so go for it. You'll pay the piper on your way out.* Whether it's some form of wealth, a "better" social image, or fitting into another social group, God knows your motivations for asking. He knows where our hearts are in relation to Him better than we do. He does well to call us adulteresses since we go courting the world in selfish pleasure and reject Him while we are asking for gifts from Him (Matthew 6:24). If we want to be friends with the world, we make ourselves enemies of God. Think about it. In the end God's enemies always lose; on the losing team is not a good place to be.

Thank God that He loves us enough to sometimes say no to our requests.

James 4:5

"Or do you think that the Scripture speaks to no purpose: 'He jealously desires the Spirit which He has made to dwell in us?'"

Hmm. But I thought jealousy was a sin.

What does *jealousy* mean? Webster gives a couple of definitions: "feeling anger, or suspicion because of someone's unfaithfulness in a relationship, or, being fiercely protective of one's rights or possessions." Our Father is fiercely protective of us, and for centuries He has proven His holy and sacrificial love for us. It is no wonder He gets jealous of the attention we give to worldly things.

James is continuing his thought from verse 4, calling us adulteresses. We, as the church, are the Bride of Christ (Revelation 21:2, 9) and Jesus is the Groom (John 3:29), her husband. Yet we continue to play the adultress and chase the world's lies and shallow promises. Sometimes our pursuit of the world is very blatant, but sometimes it takes even more devious forms. We fool ourselves if we think we're being faithful Christians while we bury ourselves in what we consider good works and forget about Jesus, our first love, our priority. The Holy Spirit is the cheated spouse. We say that we have a new love for Him, but still hold hands with sin, our ex.

In Revelation 2:1-7, the church at Ephesus had a lot going for it. God knew the church's deeds, perseverance, lack of endurance for evil men, and that it revealed false prophets. The church endured for the name of Jesus and did not grow weary. Not many modern churches can say the same. Yet, in verse 4, the Lord says the church has left her first love. How can that be? Looking at verse 5, it seems that over time the Ephesians had gotten into doing what they considered to be the work of the Lord, but without the Lord. God says "Repent and do the deeds you did at first." Doing a lot of religious stuff doesn't necessarily mean you're being obedient to the Holy Spirit. If God wants you to be on a prayer team once a week, but you feel the need to be on 15 committees for whatever reason, you're deceiving yourself.

I remember the excitement I felt when I was first born again. My love for Jesus filled every moment, every action, every thought. The joy of the Lord overwhelmed me! I prayed for wisdom. Right away I asked Jesus what it was that He wanted me to do; what was it that made Him happy? The burdens and addictions were melting away.

But what happened as time went by? Whereas once I sought the will of God for every little thing, I slowly started to rely on my own wisdom and strength and told myself if I wanted to please God more I should do more, I should "step out in faith." I began doing what I thought the Lord wanted, but not confirming it in prayer. I did some good things that looked pretty holy, and I hoped God would be pleased. But now I must confess that the biggest reason I did many of those things was for recognition from people. The approval of people was more important than the approval of God. Recognition has always been important to me. Maybe it's an insecurity thing. I confess the desire for man's approval and recognition is still sometimes what motivates me into action, not the fact that I know it may please God. I am, at these times, an adulterer in my relationship with my First Love. He is deeply jealous of my friendship, my involvement, my romance with the world, and greatly desires my return to Him. Yet, His love for me prevents Him from divorcing Himself from me. Oh, the deep, deep love of Jesus.

James 4:6-8

"But He gives a greater grace. Therefore, it says, 'God is opposed to the proud, but gives grace to the humble.' Submit therefore to God. Resist the devil and he will flee from you. Draw near to God and He will draw near to you. Cleanse your hands, you sinners; and purify your hearts, you double-minded."

What is there anywhere on earth or even in the spiritual realms that can compare with the grace so freely rained on us by our Father in Heaven? Romans 11 talks about how God's love and patience outlasts human sinfulness, though He will not strive with mankind forever (Genesis 6:3). Romans 11:33 declares that His wisdom, understanding, and judgements are beyond our comprehension. In those times when we are far away from Him, is it possible that He understands our anger, our pain, and the reasons for our lustful behavior (Hebrews 2:14-18; 4:14-16)? Where else can we go to find perfect love except to Him? His sheep know His voice. He searches for us and finds us when we wander and He never gives up on us (John 10). We cannot understand why God would continue to love us when we treat Him the way we so often do. But, thank God He does!

So, if God loves everyone so much, why does He "oppose the proud"? Remember the phrase "you can lead a horse to water, but you can't make him drink"? I can lead a man to the foot of the cross, but if he's not willing to yield his pride to Jesus and admit to God and himself that he is weak, sinful, and in need of a savior, how could he believe that Jesus could benefit him in any way? His arrogance prevents him from seeing the truth about himself. On the other hand, the humble person is more willing to see himself as a sinner in need of forgiveness and made clean in the blood of Jesus. Will we remain blind and arrogant, refusing God and His grace? Will we open our eyes, admit the truth regarding our need of the Savior and receive the indescribable loving grace of Jesus? Indeed, the humble person is the stronger and wiser of the two.

Arrogance and pride are what caused Satan to fall, and they have the same effect on us. The devil uses our pride against us; it causes us to think we are capable of saving ourselves and creating our own destiny. How can a bad tree produce good fruit? How can a sinner create a sinless, perfect paradise? It can't happen. But James tells us that if we, through the power of the Holy Spirit, make the decision to resist our enemy the devil and rely on the strength and wisdom of the Holy Spirit instead of our own strength, Satan will flee from us. Sometimes the decision to turn and fight is harder than the fight itself.

What does it look like to fight against Satan? Here comes that old, archaic word Billy Graham used so often: "repent"! It doesn't matter how good you think you are; you aren't good enough. It doesn't matter how often you go to church; it's not enough. Jesus did not come to condemn but to save the world (John 3:17). But by your own actions and rebellious nature you bring condemnation on yourself! God has already provided His Son Jesus to die as the last, best, and final sacrifice and if you fail to take advantage of His provision, you have no one to blame for your condemnation but yourself. Your way into Heaven is paid for by your faith in His blood, death, and resurrection. You must repent. The phrase "cleanse your hands" in verse 8 means to quit doing the sinful things you have been doing. The blood of Jesus will wash off the dirt. Turn your back on the old lifestyle that separated you from God and condemned you to death. Submit to God and ask Him to forgive you. Ask Jesus to enter your heart as your Lord. The Holy Spirit will then begin a miraculous work in you rebuilding you into a new person! John 14:6 says Jesus is the only way to the Father that we have. He is *the* way, *the* Truth, and *the* life. Jesus is not *a* way or *a* truth as some believe. He is the *only* way to get to God or into Heaven.

Is this issue of repentance only meant for people who are not yet Christians? No, not at all! Because of our sinful human nature, temptation is something that every person falls victim to. Many times, when we sin, we know that what we are about to do is wrong, but we do it anyway. We could have decided against the action, or chosen different words to say, but for some reason we choose to obey our sin nature in spite of the Spirit's prompting. Then we expect God to continue to bless us in spite of our actions and get depressed or mad when He doesn't. We are double-minded—we want God to bless us but at the same time we hold onto our rebellious attitude. Afterward, we may think that we crossed the line, that He doesn't love us anymore, that He left us, or maybe that we weren't really saved to begin with. The problem is not with God. Purify your hearts from doubt and unbelief. God is trustworthy. He is faithful regarding His promise never to leave us (Hebrews 13:5).

Is God's love conditional? No. God has promised so many times that He will not leave or forsake us. Yet His righteousness can in no way have fellowship with an unrepentant heart. If He continued to dwell with us while we continued to sin it would be as if He were indifferent to our sin, like He didn't care. Jesus' crucifixion would have been cruel, pointless torture serving no purpose. But our God is a loving and holy God who loves us beyond description and created us with the ability to make decisions. Will we decide to serve and live with God in His kingdom and receive all the blessings of that relationship, or will we choose to isolate ourselves from Him and lose out on His blessings? As much as we would like it to be otherwise, we can't have it both ways. Even when good things happen while we sin, it doesn't mean that the "blessing" came from God. He doesn't reward bad behavior any more than I reward my kids when they disobey. Like a human father, God cautions us, then lets us experience the fruit of our actions.

There are two keys to remember here. First, keep a humble, repentant heart. A mind focused on God and a repentant heart go hand-in-hand. Second, strive for singleness of mind. Focus your mind on God and His ways. (Matthew 6:33).

James 4:9-10

"Be miserable and mourn and weep; let your laughter be turned into mourning and your joy to gloom. Humble yourselves in the presence of the Lord, and He will exalt you."

One of the things that kept me away from Jesus for so long was the doom-and-gloom attitude of many of the Christians I saw. They were having no fun in life. The church services I attended were boring. While I didn't speak with an abnormally loud voice, I was roundly "shushed" when I spoke or greeted someone. Their songs they "sang" were more like dirges.

Is this how James is encouraging believers to behave in verse 9? Not at all. Remember that James is addressing believers who are arguing, quarrelling among themselves, and coveting what other people have. They claim Christ's name while they ask God for blessings to spend on their own pleasures. As a result, their worship of those worldly pleasures makes them proud, and they turn away from God (1 John 2:15-17). James is saying that very often, even as believers, we aren't taking the seriousness of sin to heart. As we happily play, work, or sleep our born-again lives away, are we completely ignorant of the fact that we may be wasting our lives and talents? Are we aware that perhaps death is closer than we think (Luke 12:15-21)? Oh, but for the mercies of God!

Are we so drunk on pleasure and absorbed by self-fulfillment that we think more of ourselves than we ought? Are we so discouraged with the world and our lives as we see them that we withdraw into fantasies, thinking less of ourselves that we ought? The lesson here is not to walk around with a long and gloomy look on our faces and never to have any fun. And there's nothing wrong with feeling good about yourself; after all, whose image are you created in (Genesis 1:26; 9:6; 1 Corinthians 11:7)? Being so depressed about something that we are driven to regularly fantasize about another kind of life (or even death) is a weapon used by Satan to distract us from the Truth and blind us to who we really are in Christ and how much joy there is in a Christ-centered life. Satan wants to hide from us how much joy we can bring to God with the talents He gives us when we use them with

His strength to defeat the Devil. Remember the mirror in James 1:23-24 (see also 2 Peter 1:9). If Christians start to focus again on worldly wealth instead of our riches in heaven, we will drift away from God, forgetting who we are in Christ.

I think the lesson here is to take a long, sober, objective look at yourself in relation to God's word and see where you stand, using His Word as the measuring stick. Through the Bible, you will see that you are not in control of your destiny, as so many people like to think they are. You will see that God is holy. You will see that you are a sinner and that you need a savior. And you will see that the only savior worthy of your worship is Jesus. You can then repent of your sin and humbly, yet joyfully, and enter into His presence because only at that point will you have learned what real humility is, and He will exalt you (Luke 14:11)! He will lift you up! Think about it: handing off the dead weight of all your sin; Jesus lifting it from your shoulders. Even well-conditioned hikers are relieved to get their heavy packs off their backs. How good losing that burden feels! The God of eternity, the God Who created Heaven and Earth, will lift you up and bless you as a good father loves and blesses his son or daughter!

James 4:11-12

"Do not speak against one another, brethren. He who speaks against a brother or judges his brother, speaks against the law and judges the law; but if you judge the law, you are not a doer of the law but a judge of it. There is only one Lawgiver and Judge, the One who is able to save and to destroy; but who are you who judge your neighbor?"

When you or I make a judgement of someone, or belittle them, or insult them, we don't do it to make them feel bad about themselves. I mean a good Christian just wouldn't do that, right? No, we do these things to make ourselves look or feel better (Luke 18:10-14). Even if we say we're joking, it's a power trip, an ego exercise, a pride thing common to both men and women. Call it what you want, insults never encourage or motivate anyone to be better, no matter what the intention.

The Law was given to Moses by God as the standard for living. Its purpose was to show the people their continual sinfulness and the resulting need for continual sacrifice. If the Jews were to follow these commandments, all would be well between God and mankind, as well as among the people. If they didn't, things would not go well, and blood would have to flow. For New Testament believers like you and me, Jesus was the final sacrifice for our sin, and He summarized all the Law and the Prophets with Matthew 22:36-40: "Love the Lord with all your heart, soul, and mind" and "Love your neighbor as much as yourself." Imagine what the world would be like if we all did only these two things! But that would be far too simple. We must delineate who our neighbors are, how much to love them, what is required, and how often. We decide on standards, and if you don't perform to these standards, we must assume you have backslidden, that you are hiding other sins, and do not measure up to our standards. A little hypocritical, don't you think? And, for better or for worse, this hypocrisy is not new (Matthew 7:1; 10:28; Luke 6:42).

A number of years ago my wife and I were walking downtown during farmer's market. Ahead of us a block or so was a group of young people who, to me, looked like a bunch of rowdies dressed in black, with studs in their noses, tattoos, and weird colored hair. They were playing guitars, had a bass violin and bongos, and were singing (screaming) about something. I wanted to turn around and casually go the other way, but no, my wife wanted to go and see what they were singing about. So, we did. To my embarrassment and amazement, they were singing praises to God! Shouting "Hallelujah! Praise the one Lord Jesus Christ!" Why was I amazed and embarrassed? I had automatically assumed, based on what I thought I saw and what I thought I heard from a distance, that they were screaming obscenities and violence. Judging by what they were wearing I prejudiced them to be something or someone they were not. I was condemning them when they were actually some of my brothers and sisters in Christ! They were ministering the Gospel of Jesus to a group of people like themselves, a group that people like me never could (or would care enough to) reach.

We have all sinned and continue to do so. Without the grace of God and the blood of Jesus to cleanse us from our sin by faith, we are all guilty (John 8:7; Hebrews 10:31). So, who are we to judge another person? There is only one Judge and Lawgiver, One who is able to save and destroy. How can it be that one Judge is able to both convict and defend? It's easy if our God is a triune God. God the Father holds us accountable for our sin, and God the Son speaks on our behalf saying, "Because of their faith, these are children of yours! They are innocent because My blood has removed their sin! Your Holy Spirit is a witness!" (See John 15:26 and John 16:7.) Does this sound as if there is conflict within the Godhead? Not at all. This is perfect justice executed by our perfect God. Sin is recognized by the Judge, so by the Law, sacrificial blood is required. This sin was covered (atoned for) through the blood of His Son. Because of His sacrifice, we are found innocent.

What can wash away my sin? Nothing but the blood of Jesus! Perfect justice with perfect grace.

James 4:13-17

"Come now, you who say, 'Today or tomorrow we will go to such and such a city, and spend a year there and engage in business and make a profit.' Yet you do not know what your life will be like tomorrow. You are just a vapor that appears for a little while and then vanishes away. Instead, you ought to say, 'If the Lord wills, we will live and also do this or that.' But as it is, you boast in your arrogance; all such boasting is evil. Therefore, to one who knows the right thing to do and does not do it, to him it is sin."

If we have allowed the Lord to develop within us the mindset that Jesus is, indeed, our Head and Master, and if we are, indeed, in submission to His will, then acknowledging His direction for our decisions will come more easily, almost naturally. In fact, at those times when He does thwart our plans, we should rejoice because He must have something better for us in mind. Maybe He's just keeping us alive for another day. Too often I spend my time and energy doing some things I thought were important, only to later realize they really weren't. I have found that more often than not, I don't ask God for His input or find His will regarding a project.

Our lives are just a vapor, like a puff of smoke, dust in the wind. When we look inside, we see ourselves as so much more, don't we? James is cleaning off the mirror from chapter one so we will see ourselves more clearly. Even if we don't say so, we tend to run our daily lives as if we were the masters of our own destinies as long as we live, and we usually decide not to think about the fact that we don't have control over how long our lives will be (Luke 12:16-21; Psalm 39:4-6). Life on Earth is far too short, and eternity is far too long, to live without Jesus involved.

Who do you believe the God of the Bible to be? How big is the God you serve? Everybody serves a god of some kind. We're all a slave of something. Is He bigger than you? Bigger than all your problems, worries, and concerns? All the time? Really? If I think my God is always bigger and smarter than me, I should ask for His input much more often than I do and involve Him in many more aspects of my life. I should also realize how small I am and how eternally powerful God is.

Why do we act this way, acting as if we know what's best for us (and maybe those around us) and have no need of God or His direction? James 4:16 says it is arrogance. We live out our prideful selves before God. It is evil, but how is it evil? We know we shouldn't do a certain thing, but we do it anyway (James

4:5-8; Romans 7). With our mouths we sing God's praises, but with our lives we sing our own. If you know the right thing to do (Micah 6:8) and you don't do it, it is sin (verse 17). Keep in mind, however, that you cannot push the conviction the Lord gave to you onto others as if it were their conviction as well. If, for example, the Lord has convicted you regarding drinking alcohol, you cannot force everyone else to abstain from alcohol as well. Our Father knows and cares enough about each of his kids to deal with us individually. Let Him be the one to convict your brothers and sisters in Christ.

James 5:1-6

*"Come now, you rich, weep and howl
for your miseries which are coming
upon you. Your riches have rotted
and your garments have become
moth-eaten. Your gold and your
silver have rusted; and their rust will
be a witness against you and will
consume your flesh like fire. It is in
the last days that you have stored up
your treasure! Behold, the pay of the
laborers who mowed your fields, and
which has been withheld by you, cries
out against you; and the outcry of
those who did the harvesting has
reached the ears of the Lord of
Sabaoth. You have lived luxuriously
on the earth and led a life of wanton
pleasure; you have fattened your
hearts in a day of slaughter. You
have condemned and put to death the
righteous man; he does not resist
you."*

A close friend of mine is a retired surgeon. He lives in a house that Solomon would find very comfortable. He likes buying his wife of over fifty years diamond rings—not huge ones, but nice ones. He bought lights for his pool and spa that slowly change colors. He and his wife also sincerely love Jesus and serve Him in many ways both locally and overseas. They are perfectly at peace in the knowledge that their possessions have absolutely no eternal value and they will happily leave them behind when they die and move into the place that Jesus is preparing for them in Heaven.

So, what is the difference between my friend and the rich brothers and sisters described in these verses? My friend has studied Matthew 6:19-21 and knows very well where his real treasure is: "Do not store up for yourselves treasures on earth, where moths and vermin destroy, and where thieves break in and steal. But store up for yourselves treasures in heaven, where moths and vermin do not destroy, and where thieves do not break in and steal. For where your treasure is, there your heart will be also." People that James included as "my brothers" in chapter 1:2 and 5:7 were defrauding and persecuting people around them. Their tarnished gold and silver, their expensive, moth-eaten garments and income they gained through corruption will all be evidence against them when they give their account standing before Jesus in Heaven. Their earthly treasure will burn like a bonfire in the last days (Matthew 6:19-21, Philippians 3:7-11). What they consider to be riches is cheap imitation.

God knows the heart of everyone. Whereas man may be impressed with wealth, which gives the impression of power, wisdom, or godliness, God is not. Real gold and silver do not rust. Thus, these brothers and sisters, by their sinful behavior, their wanton pleasure, have "fattened their hearts for the slaughter;" they have brought judgement upon themselves by condemning, judging, and devaluing people around them (look back at James 4:11-12; and 1 Corinthians 3:15).

Is it only the rich who devalue others? Of course not. The rich judge the poor, the poor judge the rich, the old judge the young, the young judge the old. It goes on and on and on, both inside and outside of the church. Amid all this evaluation of worth, who is this "righteous man," and why doesn't he resist the condemnation leveled at him? Jesus did not resist the lies and condemnation (Math.27:11-14) when he stood before the Pharisees and then Pilate. Jesus knew their accusations were false. I think he knew why they were bringing lies against him to Pilate—to protect themselves and their position. I think he also knew that arguing wouldn't change anything anymore than fully answering Pilate's question regarding his kingship would. Romans 12:19 has sound advice for believers who find themselves being lied about or accused falsely: let God deal with the accusers. Jeremiah 17:10 and Proverbs 3:31, 24:29, and 26:24 also address how to handle our accusers and perhaps see who this righteous man is. He is the believer who allows the Lord to defend him. Reflect again on James 1:2-5. Sometimes it takes greater strength of character and wisdom to keep our mouths shut than to rush to our own defense.

My surgeon friend knows that anything amounting to true riches comes only from above and brings glory to God, not to himself or his wife. He also knows that no amount of riches, whether from above or below, gives him the right to judge or condemn anybody for any reason because if he were to do that, he would be trying to usurp God's position of authority. That does not work out well for anyone. Reflect again on James 4:12. There is only one Lawgiver and Judge, and you aren't Him.

James 5:7-8

"Therefore, be patient, brethren, until the coming of the Lord. The farmer waits for the precious produce of the soil, being patient about it, until it gets the early and late rains. You too be patient; strengthen your hearts, for the coming of the Lord is near."

James uses the word *patient* three times in these two verses. Apparently, he thinks it's important.

Verse six ends with people living lives of wanton pleasure, fattening their hearts as for a day of slaughter, and putting to death a righteous man. Then verse seven starts by telling us to be patient. How does being patient relate with wanton (sinful) pleasure and murder?

If we live our lives focused on only satisfying our lusts (wanton pleasures) and self-fulfillment, we are completely disregarding the eternal condition of our souls. To steal a line from the Eagles, we want life in the fast lane, "everything all the time." We are provoking the sin within us. We cannot remain in this condition and also be "following the Lord." If we think this way, we are nigh to being the topic of discussion in Hebrews 6:4-8. Patience, then, is an antidote to living a life of sinful pleasure. When we patiently put our trust in Jesus, trusting in His return, we do not seek to fill our lives with empty sinful patterns.

James uses a farming analogy to illustrate patience. Before the farmer even starts waiting for the crop to grow, he prepares the soil. He plows to break the hard crust so the seed can root at the right time. He pulls and digs up the weeds that would hinder or prevent seed growth. He provides water so the young plant can grow and not die. If we put ourselves in the place of the seed, this entire sequence is the process of growing in Christ for the believer, and it lasts a lifetime. We often do not see God's mercy and compassion while in hard times, but it is evident at the end. Take heart; if we remain patient and faithful to the end, it will be worth it (Romans 8:18). Our patience and our trust in Jesus through trying times will, indeed, make our hearts strong. Remember, during any plant's life there is never a point of stasis—where it simply exists. For the plant to survive, all its physical processes must be working all the time. If it's not growing, it's dying. Something to think about when we look at the church or ourselves and serving our Lord.

Let's look at the work of this farmer again.
1. The seed is planted.
2. The seed dies to itself; it ceases to be just a seed and begins to become a plant because of the care the farmer has taken.
3. The young plant continues to grow and mature, feeding from the nutrients in the tilled soil.
4. As the plant matures it begins to bear fruit. The farmer prunes away branches that are not bearing so that the plant won't waste energy by putting it into unproductive branches.

From a spiritual perspective:
1. Someone tells us the Gospel of Christ.
2. We die to ourselves; we repent of our sins and give our lives to Jesus. We cease living only to satisfy our own lusts and begin to live for Jesus through serving Him by using the wisdom and gifts the Lord has put into each one of us.
3. As we grow and push our roots deeper into His Word, we gain stability and strength and begin to blossom.
4. As we mature in Him (regardless of our chronological age), we begin to bear spiritual fruit—living out the fruits of the Spirit in Galatians 5:22-25. The Lord prunes the areas of our lives that hinder us from bearing more fruit (Psalm 94:12, 118:16-18, John15:2-5, Hebrews 12:5-11). Often this is where our pride and rebellious spirits come into play. At this point we need to slow down, trust God, be patient, and perhaps return to James chapter one. God will cut away the desires, habits, and fears that prevent us from being most fully yielded to Him.

While we are like the seed, being tended to by the Farmer, James also compares us to a farmer. Like the farmer, we have no control over the weather and must patiently trust God to provide the sun and rain necessary to grow the crops. We should be patient and meanwhile strengthen our hearts by praying and looking to the Lord for guidance.

Don't we take comfort in knowing that He is coming soon to collect us up to be with Him? Aren't we encouraged in knowing that He will never leave us or forsake us? And that we will never be tested beyond our capability when we abide in Christ? That's how our hearts are strengthened—by resting in Jesus, having the courage to stand still and not strive after or worry about things as they confront us. If we are not patient, how can we rest in Him and believe that He will take care of us? Either we believe He will and rest in that, or we don't believe and continue to get stressed out. Scientific research has told us that stress can cause heart disease. Isn't it interesting that science has also documented that people who pray or have some form of religious belief suffer less from stress than those who have no religious belief system? How much more comforting should it be to know that we can have not a religious belief system, but a personal relationship with the eternal God of all creation, who loves us with an indescribable love! Jesus longs to be intimately involved in our daily lives if we simply ask Him and believe He will do what He has said. How much do we actually believe that? Enough to ask and trust?

James 5:9-11

*"Do not complain, brethren,
against one another, so that you
yourselves may not be judged;
behold, the Judge is standing right
at the door. As an example,
brethren, of
suffering and patience, take the
prophets who spoke in the name of
the Lord. We count those blessed
who endured. You have heard of
the endurance of Job and have
seen the outcome of the Lord's
dealings, that the Lord is full of
compassion and is merciful."*

The prophets, such as Ezekiel, Jeremiah, Samuel, and others, loved God dearly and served Him faithfully. But they were often brutally persecuted. They had their property and belongings stolen and family members murdered or beaten. Some of the apostles were hanged, beheaded, stoned, or sawn in half. Believers today, in some parts of the world, are still persecuted in much the same way because they love and serve Jesus. In spite of these atrocities, the church continues to grow and become stronger because their Message and their acts of love are more important than the cost. Ours is a spiritual battle that began in Eden and will continue until the Lord returns. You and I are not isolated victims when bad things happen to us. Our enemy, Satan, hates us beyond measure and knows his time is short. Our choice is to serve our selfish pride—thus surrendering to Satan—or to remain faithful (have patience) through the battle and gain the victory through Jesus and His work of faith on the cross.

One way we live out patient faithfulness to Jesus is by being patient with other believers. Complaints about others are judgments we make against others. Judging others is not our job. Jesus is standing right there at the door, and He can see the situation much more clearly than we can. He is the Judge, not us, and He is most concerned with the truth regarding people's hearts, rather than how they appear. The Holy Spirit will convict them if they need it, so we don't have to. He may even be using them to work on you and your attitude and character.

How do people develop strong, godly character? We don't. Let's rephrase the question: How does God develop a strong, godly character in us? By giving us everything we ask for? By isolating us from all trouble? Many Christians seem to think so, but muscles get strong when they are given the right nutrition and when they exercise against resistance. Likewise, feed on the Word of God, and He will provide the opportunities for spiritual exercise. Christlike character gets stronger when our faith, morality, and intellect are challenged. When others attack your faith and you remain faithful, when you defend what you believe is right in the marketplace, when you stand up for the defenseless, and when you feed the hungry—all in the name of Jesus—God is building a powerful character inside you (Philippians 2:13). Your strength is built not through anything you have done, but through God, who is at work within you (Philippians 1:6, Ephesians 2:9).

James says, "We count those blessed who endured." But today, do we consider it a blessing to endure suffering for being faithful? Let's pause for a minute and remember what we talked about in chapter one. Tribulation makes us stronger in Jesus. Our eyes are on ourselves when we focus on the immediate pain or difficulty, but when we raise our eyes up to Him, our point of view and our priorities change. When was the last time I quietly sat and meditated on the depth of Job's suffering and what it produced? In all my spiritual prowess, the last time I thought about the outcome of his suffering, I was quick to point out that he got all his stuff back and let it go at that. But, according to Scripture, Job got back much more than just his belongings. (And, by the way, Job's story does not guarantee that we would get back our stuff back if we were in the same situation. Getting our stuff back is not the point.) Even though God already considered him to be a righteous man, Job gained a peace and depth of relationship with God that he could never have had without the complete loss of everything around him. Though Job was a godly man before his ordeal, he was a much stronger man afterward.

I think today, especially in our western, post-modern culture, we see suffering from a different perspective than God does, or even how we saw it a hundred years ago. Are we, as a world population, being punished? What was it that we did wrong? Obviously, we must not be able (or willing) to fix *it* because we can't even agree what *it* is... and what we're really wondering is why *those* people won't agree with us? Funny how *those* people are asking the same thing. Sad how God is asking the same thing, all the while knowing the answer. An addict finds it difficult to admit he has a problem, and when someone who cares for him points it out, he may get defensive and angry. Are we, as a world population, addicted to our sin? Do we get defensive when someone who cares for us points it out and offers a solution and a cure? Alcoholics and drug addicts often find it uncomfortable to be around people who are not addicts. Having been one of those, I know. I also know that people were often uncomfortable around me.

When I discovered that someone who cared was offering another option, I had to first admit to myself that my solutions to my problems were not working. At first, I got defensive. *Are we pawns in some galactic chess game? It's not our fault the world is circling the toilet. Yeah, that's it! We're victims! Victims of the Fates. There are stronger forces out there and no matter what we do it changes nothing. It's not our fault! So just be a good person and hope that death comes quietly in the night.*

Eventually, I was willing to listen and look. Well, it is our fault that the world is in the shape it's in, and yes, there are stronger forces out there, but we are failing or refusing to grow up and take responsibility for making our world and our personal lives the way they are. We see only a tiny, microscopic snapshot of a gigantic panorama, like a grain of sand at the bottom of the Grand Canyon. What God allows us to go through is always for His glory, for our benefit, to build us up in Christ, and to always bring us into a much more personal and intimate love relationship with Him (James 1:2-3). That is why people who faithfully endure their hardship are blessed. That is why we can rejoice in our tribulations. Those pains can never compare with the glorious peace of knowing Jesus and the reward waiting for us in Heaven (Philippians 3:7-10).

Even so, come quickly Lord Jesus.

James 5:13-15

"Is any among you afflicted? Let him pray. Is any merry? Let him sing psalms. Is anyone among you sick? Then he must call for the elders of the church and they are to pray over him, anointing him with oil in the name of the Lord; and the prayer offered in faith will restore the one who is sick, and the Lord will raise him up, and if he has committed sins, they will be forgiven him."

Have you heard someone say, "I swear on a stack o' Bibles 30 feet high it's the truth!" or something like that? Have you told someone that you would do something, and received the reply, "Do you promise?"

Why does James say now not to swear by Heaven or earth or any other oath? Because the words that come out of our mouths reveal who we are inside. If we are practicing what James and the rest of Scripture teaches, then the words coming from our mouths will evidence integrity, honesty, and steadfast character. There is therefore no need for emotional, passionate oaths. Don't make a production of it, simply say "Yes, I will do it," then do it, or "No, I won't do that," and then don't do it. If this is how you do things, there is no need for people to ask if you promise because they know you are good for your word.

Since we were relocated out of Eden, we have been searching. Searching for something safe. Searching for something dependable, something stable. Something made of truth and understanding. Something forgiving, yet that holds us accountable. Something that proves our lives are worthwhile and have meaning. But some*thing* is not what we need. What we need is some*one*. If we are honest, not one of us can name a person we have known that perfectly fit that bill. No wife, no husband, no friend. Jesus Christ, the Son of God, is the only person in the history of humanity who perfectly fills that void in us and every other, every time, with no exceptions.

So, what does all this have to do with swearing? As Christians, we are what someone called "windows to God." I have also heard us called "the only Jesus some people will ever see." People see God as they see us. That's a scary thought to some people, and maybe it should be to others. I think the issue in verse 12 is integrity. The world is searching for a group of trustworthy people, where integrity is common between all members. Proverbs 23:7 says, "as a man thinks, so he is." If you memorize Scripture, it will define how you do things. It will change how you speak. It will become your nature. It will be what others see through you. It will help prevent you from falling "under [the] judgement" of other people watching you (verse 12). Your words and actions build your reputation. When people see you, do they see a person who says one thing, but does another, who is not dependable or trustworthy? Or do they speak highly of you because they know that you are honorable and good for your word? As you study Scripture, God will be causing the fruit of the Spirit to grow within you (Galatians 5:22). Your changed behavior and lifestyle will be strong evidence of God's ability to change lives. Godly integrity is a sign of being at peace with not only God, but also with yourself. When our reputation includes this godly integrity, we don't have to swear these extreme oaths because our character and actions will reflect God's faithfulness through us.

While the word James used for "swear" primarily means promise, as moderns, we have taken it to a whole other level. Contemporary Christians have made light of common profane swearing, but I believe we need to take it more seriously. Profanity gives no eternal gain, gives no encouragement, and damages our Christian testimony and credibility. Need an example? There's nothing holy about the phrase "Holy crap." You use the same word to describe our God and feces and you think that's okay? Stop saying it. What about, "Oh my God" or "OMG"? Unless you're willing to finish this exclamation with something like "You're so great and full of mercy!" choose another way to express your thoughts without sounding like the world (Ephesians 4:29). Neither your constitutional freedom of speech nor your freedom in Christ give you permission to offend people by the content of your speech or profanity. "Oh, it's just a saying," you might think, "Nobody is offended by it. Don't get so upset!" Even if the people around you don't seem to be offended by it, what if God is offended by it? We have become desensitized to sin. We want to sound like the world so that we'll fit into a place that we, as followers of Jesus, no longer belong. We want to get as close to sin as we can because then we'll fit in with a sinful society, but not actually sin because we think that would make God... sad or something.

Words build worlds. Use your words to build a world where the love of Jesus is spoken visibly over every border and within every church.

James 5:16-19

"Therefore, confess your sins to one another, and pray for one another so that you may be healed. The effective prayer of a righteous man can accomplish much. Elijah was a man with a nature like ours, and he prayed earnestly that it would not rain, and it did not rain on the earth for three years and six months. Then he prayed again, and the sky poured rain and the earth produced its fruit."

Pain is the body's way of telling us that something is wrong, both in our individual physical bodies and within the body of Christ, the church. James encourages believers to see pain, affliction, and illness as reminders to turn in prayer to the source of our strength.

When we are in pain, Jesus prays to His Father for us, although perhaps not in the same way we might pray. In Luke 22:31, we learn Satan demanded permission to "sift" Peter, to put him through some really hard times. Instead of asking God to stop Satan or spare Peter from the pain, which I think many of us would have done, Jesus prayed that Peter's "faith would not fail." He then urged Peter to "go and strengthen the brothers" after he came through the trial. We, like Peter, are to share with fellow Christians the same strength and comfort that we receive from God during trials.

Paul described this strengthening when Titus came to him in 2 Corinthians 7:6-7. Because Titus was comforted by the church at Corinth, he was able to give Paul much comfort and joy during his visit. The experience we gain when we go through trials is not always for our benefit alone, but for the building up of other believers around us and for the testimony of the power of Christ to weak or unbelieving people as well. It's not all about me! How can we encourage other Christians to persevere through trials if we ourselves are unwilling to do the same? How can we persevere through trials without the strength of the Lord? How better to trust His strength than through prayer?

Here in chapter 5:14-15, James mentions a possible connection between sickness and sin. Look at the progression from verse 14 through 15. Anyone who is sick must call for the elders, who will pray over him, anointing him with oil in the name of the Lord. Their prayer offered in faith will restore the one who is sick, and the Lord will raise him up, and if the sick person has committed sin, he will be forgiven. Confess your sins to one another and pray for each other so that you will be healed. Does this mean illness is always the result of sin? No. The passage doesn't say that sin caused the disease. Is sin-induced illness possible? Yes, but don't believe that if someone is sick it's only because of unconfessed sin. The point is that during a time of sickness, or any affliction, is when the heart is most receptive to the Holy Spirit's ministry, and the best way to participate with the Spirit is through prayer.

The anointing with oil is a symbol of the presence of the Holy Spirit. It represents God's cleansing of us, our being re-equipped for His service. Anointing with oil reminds us again of His divine favor toward us (1 John 1:9). The emphasis is on God, and His healing action, not the oil (Philippians 2:13).

The prayers mentioned in this passage are clearly spoken aloud, since they are spoken in a group. Of course, whether we pray quietly or aloud, God still hears us. In one of my darkest times, I whispered songs and prayers to God in the dark. Even though I was alone I could not bring myself to speak aloud, but I knew He heard me.

Silent prayer has its place, but it's also true that praise was meant to be verbally, physically expressed. I think it is sad when God has done something wonderful in our lives that brings us so much joy, and we keep it to ourselves. Why do we do this? Because we don't want to look silly? When my sons played youth soccer and scored a goal I jumped around like a crazy man! Praise is a natural response to feeling good about something. When each of my boys were born, I was ecstatic! When I had cancer and the surgery went so well, I was so blessed! When we feel alone yet know He is with us, we should sing! If you don't think that you can sing, that's okay. God, who created you and loves you, would still love to hear your voice! Read through Psalms and count all the times David and the other authors encourage us to praise the Lord with our voices and instruments. Even in his most desperate times, David prayed and praised God. David might not have been glad he was hiding in a cave, but he knew God was his shield and protector. Instead of keeping our hands in our pockets and letting our eyes roam around the church, we should sing our songs up to God! The joy of the Lord is our strength! Give the credit where it is due. Tell God how much you love Him, how you appreciate Him, how grand and wonderful He is, how you are so blessed by what He has done, how much you need Him and love to serve Him. Praise is food for your spirit and lifts your soul, strengthening you for the seasons of sickness and affliction.

James 5:19-20

"My brethren, if any among you strays from the truth and one turns him back, let him know that he who turns a sinner from the error of his way will save his soul from death and will cover a multitude of sins."

James points out that confession to others builds account-ability between believers and therefore increases the depth of our prayers. As long as we're talking about confessing our sins, I'll confess this—it's a lot easier for me to confess my sins to God quietly and in private than it is for me to confess them to another person—even a close friend. Why is that you ask? Well, my pride is massive. I don't want people knowing the things I struggle with (over and over) even if I know they deal with the same struggles (1 Corinthians 10:13). Oh, but I'm fine if they want to confess their sins to me because I want to look like a mature, faithful brother that they can come to... yeah, hypocrit-ical I confess.

There are at least two reasons why we should confess our sins to each other. First, I can turn my pride into a motivating force; if I have to tell someone that I have sinned yet again, maybe I'll put more energy into resisting the temptation or the sin. Secondly, resisting the urge to sin using the strength of the Holy Spirit and not my own strength, my faith will become more massive than my pride (James 1:3). I'm learning to practice what I preach.

Find someone you can trust, someone with a good relation-ship with Jesus, walking closely with Him in obedience, justified in Christ by faith, who firmly believes in the power of prayer, and who will earnestly plead for God to intercede on your behalf. James says prayer that comes before God in this way accom-plishes much, which makes sense when we think back to chapter one (1:6-8) and the double-minded person who doesn't receive anything from God because of unbelief.

Because we are in a spiritual battle with prayer as our greatest weapon, our prayer lives should be FIT: Focused, Intelligent, and Thorough. A FIT prayer is focused on an issue or a person. It is intelligent, meaning it comes from being informed. Instead of simply saying, "Oh Lord, bless the people who were hit by the hurricane," become informed about their needs and pray accordingly. A FIT prayer is also thorough, thinking through different needs. How do you want God to bless them? Keep in mind He may choose to bless them by having you physically rise from your prayer couch and serve them soup. He may have you share the Gospel on the street downtown or become involved in rescuing victims of sex-trafficking or provide safe-houses to battered women. You could become a dependable friend or mentor to an at-risk kid.

To illustrate that "an effective prayer of a righteous man can accomplish much," James says that Elijah, the prophet, was just like us, a common person who truly believed God. In 1 Kings 17 the Lord told Elijah, who then prophesied to Ahab, that because of the sins of the people and kings of Israel there would be no rain for three and a half years. For a society dependent on agriculture, and thus on rainfall, this was bad. Elijah was informed and aware of their idolatry and therefore able to offer an *intelligent* prayer. When he prayed (1 Kings 18) he was *focused*. Finally, according to what God had shown him, Elijah boldly and *thoroughly* prayed as led by God: "O Lord, the God of Abraham, Isaac and Israel, today let it be known that You are God in Israel and that I am Your servant and I have done all these things at Your word. Answer me, O Lord, answer me, that this people may know that You, O Lord, are God, and that You have turned their heart back again" (1 Kings 18:36-37).

When Elijah prayed this prayer, God responded in the exact way the people at that time and place needed. Verses 38-39 say, "Then the fire of the Lord fell and consumed the burnt offering and the wood and the stones and the dust, and licked up the water that was in the trench. When all the people saw it, they fell on their faces; and they said, 'The Lord, He is God; the Lord, He is God.'"

We seriously underestimate the power of prayer—of *our* prayer. Elijah was in a dangerous, life-threatening position, yet he prayed aloud in the presence of all the Baal worshippers that the Lord God Himself would show His glory and power to the people He loved and wanted back because their sin had separated them from Him. The "righteous man" James refers to isn't righteous because of some kind of good works. This righteous person is righteous because of faith in Jesus; because of believing what He says.

Need something to pray about, someone to pray for? Pray for your country's rulers. Pray for your local officials. Pray for the school system and your church. Pray for your neighbors. Every person on Earth needs to humble themselves, pray, seek God's face, and repent turning from their wicked ways. Our rulers are not the problem or the solution. The problem is sin. The solution is Jesus. The result is peace with God.

James 5:12

"But above all, my brethren, do not swear, either by heaven or by earth or with any other oath; but your yes is to be yes, and your no, no, so that you may not fall under judgment."

Throughout his letter, James has been teaching us what it means to persevere through trials, develop strong faith, and love and serve God. I think that it's proper he concludes with this sentence regarding straying from the truth and turning sinners from the error of their ways. What better example of showing the love of God than to get beside a brother or sister who has wandered away from Jesus or is in a time of doubt, "straying from the truth." As the Lord leads you, help them in their trials, listen as they tell you what's going on, pray with and for them, and lead them away from their sins and back to the Lord.

It happens to all of us for various reasons and lengths of time; we fall victim to our own lusts and weaknesses—maybe physical or relational desires, material wealth, jealousy or envy, etc. We try to hide our sin from people by saying everything is fine when it's not. When a faithful brother or sister loves me enough to step up and encourage me to repent from some sinful activity and I do, I can remember that, through using my friend, Jesus has saved my soul from death and my multitude of sins will be forgiven.

Sometimes when we go through extended trials and times of weakness in our faith, church is the last place we want to be. The thought of having happy Christians all around is less than appealing. We might begin to wonder if we were ever really born again, if God cares at all, or if He is really there. It is also at these times that Satan divides and conquers. We are most easily picked off and dragged away when we are separated from the rest of the group. It is also at these times, when we feel furthest from God, that we must look for Him the hardest and run to the fortress of fellowship. Those in the fortress must reach out to us with listening ears, support, prayer, and, especially, Scripture. Compassionate Christians cannot simply leave us alone because that's what we say we want or because they don't want to get involved or know what to say (James 2:15-20). Don't abandon your wounded.

Unfortunately, there are people—seemingly faithful, active, true Christians—who rebel against God, utterly rejecting His grace and mercies, and return to a life away from Him. This is different from just having doubts and some hard times. These people willfully decide to reject their faith and rationalize their sinful behavior after having experienced God's grace and love firsthand. Perhaps a person's growing doubts or newfound "facts" now outweigh their former beliefs regarding Jesus, His ministry, His crucifixion, resurrection, or their own concept of sin. Perhaps at one point they thought the Lord was asking them to do something they considered beyond reason. Perhaps they found themselves in a situation they thought God should not have allowed. Their actions say that the Gospel, Christ's death on the cross, His resurrection and subsequent victory over death, was not powerful enough or ineffective (Hebrews 6:5-6). If this was not enough proof of God's love for them, I wonder what "enough" would look like. What more could have been done? Given the violence Jesus was subjected to, I refuse to imagine what else could have been inflicted upon Him. But, to them, at this point it's not about Jesus at all. It's all about them, isn't it? No wonder Hebrews says it's impossible to "restore them again to repentance." Why would they want to? They've created their own destiny, their own future.

But don't give up too quickly on those brothers or sisters who have deserted their faith. I think that if your friend is going to walk away because of a change in attitude toward Jesus, let your friend be the one to leave, not you. Don't add fuel to their reasons for leaving Jesus because it seemed to them you didn't really care for them anyway. Love them to the end. If you have the water of life and don't try to give it to them, how is that showing the love of Christ that's living in you (James 2:17-19)?

It's not our call when to stop loving them or praying for them. Someday you might be in a similar situation and need a little encouragement yourself.

Conclusion

It's one thing to appear calm when going through trials, but it's quite another to rejoice in them. James wrote to people of the early Christian church who were going through heavy affliction and persecution. He wrote to encourage them from the words of God and their own experience that these trials would reveal the strength and source of their faith by which they were saved. They needed to have patience and trust and know that God would see them get through it all.

Today, we are no different. In our modern culture we tend to search for quick and easy ways to get out of trying times. But when the hardship continues, our faith, our trust in Jesus, can become unsteady and weak. We wonder what's going on; we lose our footing and become unstable in all our ways.

As Peter did when he stepped out of the boat and began to walk on the water, we need to keep our eyes focused on the Perfecter of our faith and keep on walking in spite of the opposition. When Peter lost his focus and looked at the waves around him, he began to sink just like we do when we concentrate on our circumstances rather than on Jesus, who has already overcome them.

Our faith is forged strong through fire. Like iron sharpens iron, other brothers and sisters in Christ are needed to hold us up in prayer and, in love, hold us accountable so that we are indeed found faithful and stronger when the trials are over.

Remember who you are in Christ. You are a new creation. The Holy Spirit, the third Person of the Trinity, is alive in you. Have the same confidence in Him as He has in you. God, your Father created you and He knows what you are capable of when you trust Him because it is actually Him who is working through you.

Be patient. Trust Jesus.

Rejoice when the tough stuff comes.

Saddle up, because it is coming.

CPSIA information can be obtained
at www.ICGtesting.com
Printed in the USA
JSHW060015091222
34535JS00004B/11

9 781662 853388